THE THINK BIG MANIFESTO

Think you can't change your life (and the world)? Think again.

THE THINK BIG MANIFESTO

Michael Port

with

Mina Samuels

WILEY

John Wiley & Sons, Inc.

For general information on our other products and services or for technical support, please contact our Customer Care Department within the United States at (800) 762-2974, outside the United States at (317) 572-3993 or fax (317) 572-4002.

Wiley also publishes its books in a variety of electronic formats. Some content that appears in print may not be available in electronic books. For more information about Wiley products, visit our web site at www.wiley.com.

Library of Congress Cataloging-in-Publication Data:

Port, Michael, 1970-

The think big manifesto : think you can't change your life (and the world) think again / Michael Port with Mina Samuels.

p. cm.

ISBN 978-0-470-43237-2 (cloth)

1. Achievement motivation. 2. Performance. I. Samuels, Mina. II. Title.

BF503.P57 2009

158—dc22

2008052145

Printed in the United States of America

10 9 8 7 6 5 4 3 2 1

We are more than we know.

We can do more with less than we think.

We (and that means *you*, too) will think bigger
about who we are and what we offer.

But this big thinking must happen now;
today, tomorrow, and forevermore.

For Jake

CONTENTS

0.
WE ARE MORE THAN WE KNOW

We will think bigger about who we are and what we offer the world.

Who *are* we?

All of us. Any of us. People you may never have heard of and many you have. The people in these pages and thousands upon thousands more.

You.

Stay-at-home mom Beryl founded a nonprofit to bring seniors and students together to enrich education.

Mike left his job as a computer salesman to take up acupuncture, founding a reproductive health and wellness center with locations across the country.

Lisa lost her husband, her job, her home, her dog, and her health in a 10-month period, but not her hope. Now she coaches other women on achieving their dreams.

Ron grew up in foster care, did a stint on the streets, and then he made his way into founding a suite of real estate industry businesses.

Brian, a 19-year-old high school dropout, bought a beat-up junk truck and founded what is now a $100 million junk collection company.

Community activist and filmmaker Annie posted a 20-minute animated film on the impact of our consumer-driven society on the Internet and became an environmental maverick.

Meeting with little success as an actor, Paul founded a program that uses the performing arts to empower teens to become leaders and activists in their communities.

Kimberly rose above a streetwise childhood and petty drug dealing to write inspirational rap and helped make a documentary film on Hurricane Katrina.

After a multiyear hiatus from a moderately successful acting career in secondary roles, Daniel landed a leading role on a prime-time TV show.

Joseph trains the leaders of some of the largest multinationals—in the collaborative power of love and having an open heart.

In a male-dominated business world of *I, me, mine*, Melani helps powerful women own their instinct to be collaborative, to include others in their success.

Jeremy transformed himself from supersuccessful hedge fund manager to organic cattle farmer and philanthropist.

Heather and Lori, who had no baking or restaurant experience, started a cupcake bakery. Three locations and 50 staff later, they're just warming up.

Brandon and Nicole had to sleep in the first of what is now a string of "Best in Dallas" yoga studios.

Alexis left a big law firm and founded her own practice, which changed industry standards in client service and estate planning.

Casey is a rebel therapist working to change the poverty identity and improve public perception of her profession.

Amanda opened her own business, and when her abusive husband continued his unsupportive ways, she left him.

Shel saved a mountain.

Jonathan created an online financial planning system.

Sandra discovered a new field of human behavior.

Another Sandra fought back against her scoliosis to cycle and ski again.

Lou founded an online association in his field.

Kody helps people become *card senders*.

Mike advises businesses on innovation opportunities.

John guides people on becoming healthy high achievers.

Tina works with virtual businesses to build their systems, teams, and product development cycles.

Debra finally stopped taking jobs that made her unhappy and now runs her own health and wellness coaching practice.

And, then there's me, Michael Port—I stopped playing it safe and wrote this book.

I.
YOU SAY
YOU WANT A
REVOLUTION

No. Definitely not. I can't write this book. Nobody is interested in these wacky, out-there ideas. They sound extreme, even radical. My book won't be good enough. And even if it is, I don't want to write a self-help book. I don't want to be thought of as some pseudo-spiritual, anti-intellectual, wannabe motivational guru. I want to write a smart book that challenges its readers to think (and one that my father will approve of). But people (agents, publishers, booksellers, and book buyers) only want easy-fix books, so what's the point? And, hey, I've already written three successful business books. Do I really want to risk my reputation on this one? And, do I really have more to say that's worth reading?

That's me—thinking small.

All of us think small thoughts from time to time or maybe even more often than that. But all of us have the potential to think big much if not most of the time. And it is about time we started doing so. No more excuses. I, for one, have stopped making excuses for myself. I finally wrote this book.

The Think Big Manifesto has been a long time coming. I held back. I waited for something I might never have recognized. I thought it was not time, that my ideas were not important. I wanted to do the book perfectly or not at all. Even though I am the leader of the Think Big Revolution, like everyone, I get sucked into thinking small. And I think that is natural.

Oh, you haven't heard of the Think Big Revolution? You will. Do you think that sounds arrogant or delusional? It's neither. It's me thinking big, yes, and seeing the future for what it can be, not getting bogged down by the past. So, what is this Think Big Revolution and who am I to be leading it?

THE THINK BIG REVOLUTION (AND ME)

One evening, years ago, I was brainstorming with some other business consultants. We were all throwing out ideas about how we wanted to brand ourselves. When I was put on the spot, I said the first thing that came to my mind, "I'm the guy to call when you're tired of thinking small." The entire room became silent, until one of the women said, "Yes, that is so you!" Still, I immediately second-guessed myself, worrying that the tagline sounded too cheesy, stupid, arrogant, or worse, wasn't true.

Yet the more I floated the phrase to others, the more positive the response was. "You make us feel capable of doing bigger things," people said. "That's why we hang around you." I had never fully realized the impact I was having on other people. It created a cycle of accountability. If they were relying on me to inspire them to think bigger, then I needed to keep on thinking bigger. Until then, I had always tried to think big in my life—not that it wasn't a challenge, not that sometimes I didn't think small. But if other people were looking to me for their motivation to think big, it made it all the more important that I keep working hard at thinking big in my own life. Because my big thinking wasn't just about me, nor should it be. Thinking big is about me, you, and so many other people—reaching out, inspiring and being inspired, and working together to meet the challenges of our times, to make change, and to create new opportunities.

An important point—so I'll repeat it right away—is that I do not think big every day. I can't. It's unlikely anyone could live by this manifesto every moment. But I try. This is not just our manifesto, the manifesto of everyone who is and wants to think big, it's my personal manifesto, too. I want to live by this every day. And although it's unlikely I can live up to quite that standard every minute, publishing this manifesto and leading the Think Big Revolution are ways to hold myself to the standard of thinking big. Just as important, or even more so, to me is that I will help others think big. My (not so) secret hope is that my son Jake will read this manifesto one day (when he's learned to read) and that he'll live by it, thinking as big as he can about what he has to offer the world.

This is how I became accountable to thinking big. I began hosting a weekly telephone call in which people could come together and share the challenges and successes of thinking big. The number of participants multiplied exponentially, expanding beyond the borders of the United States. Soon the call was so big that I started to call it a revolution to reflect the enormous collaborative power that was being unleashed by the ever-increasing numbers of people who had experienced their own personal revolution from small thinking to big thinking and were now working together with others. Already, the ThinkBigRevolution.com is an online (and offline) social networking community with thousands of members and growing bigger every day.

This manifesto is part of that revolution. Reading this is one piece of a larger puzzle. To get the whole picture you need to get online and become involved. At ThinkBig Revolution.com you'll find revolutions in progress that you can join—issues like health, wealth, spirit, money, business, fitness, psychology, leadership, and creativity. Revolutions led by some of the most forward-thinking leaders of our time. Maybe you'll be one of them. Nothing there that interests you? Start your own revolution. Bring people together around the issue that challenges you.

> It's all about thinking BIGGER about who you are and what you OFFER the world—so start offering the world bigger things in the form of a new REVOLUTION in progress.

ThinkBigRevolution.com is just the starting point, a place where you'll get comfortable mingling with other big thinkers. Your town hall or any other online or offline community and networking location may be the next good place to share your big thinking and encourage others to join the revolution. But you've got to start somewhere. And, this manifesto is your ticket, backstage pass, and handbook. Membership is free; it will always be. No one owns big thinking. Try it right now.

Yes, now.

Go to ThinkBigRevolution.com and become a Revolutionary.

I'll wait here.

. . .

. . .

You're back. That's great. Onward.

Now that you are tuned in, you are going to start seeing a lot more of that word—*revolution*. It reflects the mood of many in our country. As Toni Morrison wrote in a 2008 letter to the country, ". . . [T]his is one of those singular moments that nations ignore at their peril. I will not rehearse the multiple crises facing us, but of one thing I am certain: this opportunity for a national evolution (*even revolution*) will not come again soon" [my italics].

Revolution is more than just a political necessity. It is a personal necessity.

REVOLUTION is about one person at a time experiencing their own personal EMPOWERMENT against an existing, deficient (small thinking) system. The deficient system may be something as big as a whole political SYSTEM, or more local, like the system of a family, job, or relationship structure. It may just be the way you think about YOURSELF and your capabilities.

Any revolution, global, local, or personal, is about being fully self-expressed in the face of all the forces that conspire to pacify your drive, your hunger to be the most you can be. At first, others may not even know about your revolution. It starts inside you. And that's how it should be. This is your revolution—to think bigger about yourself and what you are capable of. Yet it is inevitable that your transformation will set an example for others. The rest is organic. As people experience personal revolutions, they will join with others to bring about bigger, more sweeping changes. Although this revolution will start with each one of us changing the way we think, this is not a revolution about individual thinking and personal success (though you will achieve more than you imagined possible when you start thinking big); this is a revolution that will bring us together to achieve something even bigger—the changes we need to make a better world.

Like the term *revolution*, *think big* is a phrase we're seeing a lot of now. Kevin Costner's film, *Swing Vote*, imagined the ideal political candidate as a *big thinker*.

It's even showing up in obituaries. Dr. Julius Richmond, who died in July 2008, accomplished many great things during his lifetime. Among them were founding Head Start, perhaps one of the most successful social programs in the country, which provides educational day care for preschoolers from poor families; testifying in class action suits by plaintiffs who developed lung cancer from secondhand smoke; and taking a stand for gay rights. In lauding his accomplishments, his obituary concluded with these words: "He thought big." Indeed he did. He started revolutions and rallied others around critical issues.

That's what the Think Big Revolution is about.

THE THINK BIG MANIFESTO

This book is the manifesto of the Think Big Revolution. You might think that word, *manifesto*, sounds quaint, or worse—dense and overwhelming, but it has never been more apt (and though this book deals with some heavy issues, it does so with lightness).

We live in challenging times. Often, the world seems a dark and dangerous place, with little hope: We are at war; there is an environmental crisis looming on the horizon; too many people live in poverty; our health care system is failing; intolerance and hatred toward others with different points of view continue to plague us; and the insidious effects of racism have yet to be eliminated. Sure, we always want to improve our personal lives, but we want more than that. We are looking, too, for a way to understand our place in the larger world and to tap the power we possess to change not only ourselves, but also the community we live in. We are hungry to belong. We want to feel that we are part of something bigger than ourselves, that what we do individually matters and has an effect in a larger sense. The television show *Heroes* has been the biggest new hit in the past five years. Its tagline? "Save the cheerleader, save the world."

The idea of one person at a time, of one person making a difference, is what we are looking for right now. You don't need to wait until you've made your millions at Google to change the world. (Actually, the folks at Google *did* change the world.) You can do it now (just as there's no sense in waiting until you've lost the weight to start your exercise regimen). We, each of us, can make a difference. Only a manifesto truly responds to our desire to make the best of our world. If *we* don't change the world, who is going to? And if we want to change the world, we need to start with ourselves. And if we change ourselves, changing the world will start to come naturally.

In these pages is a *personal* manifesto for thinking bigger about who we are and what we offer the world. It's a *professional* manifesto, too, of course. After all, your profession is as much a part of your hopes and dreams as your personal life, or it should be if you're thinking big. Even more, here is a *political* manifesto for doing big things with others. No, this has nothing to do with politics as we know it (red states and blue states and all that noise). Before politics became a dirty word, tarnished by an endless stream of self-interested power seekers feeding at a trough of money and influence, it meant something noble. Plato's politics described the process by which groups make decisions. This is a manifesto in that Platonic tradition—one of collaboration, of politics in the best and most effective sense. It is not about one person thinking big alone on the secluded island of their dreams. It is about one person thinking big and showing family and friends and colleagues and others how to think big, and on it goes.

Inspiring others **to think big is perhaps the single most important act of any one individual thinking big.**

As you think bigger, you will necessarily bring others into the fold. To think big is to desire above all else to help others to think bigger about themselves and what they can do in the world. The Think Big Revolution is about coming together with others to do big things in the world. It is about building a community founded on big thinking. Now.

II.
THIS THING CALLED
THINKING BIG

To think big is to know what we stand for and let it guide us in everything we do; to maintain our integrity in the face of a world filled with slack thinking, lazy habits, and flexible principles; to imagine the possibilities of the world and go out and do them—build a business, green the environment, rid the streets of crime, reengineer the foster care system, write a novel, run a marathon, protect animal rights, raise a child, become a vegetarian, join a nonprofit board, fight hunger and poverty, redesign our educational system, foster a peaceful and tolerant community, and the list never ends.

To think big is a personal thing, and it's a global thing.

Thinking big is not about accumulating—possessions, fame, friends, or influence. It is not about getting rich (though you may reap financial rewards). Thinking big is creating a world of collaboration and cooperation instead of competition. To think big is to build a life in which more is accomplished with others than could have been dreamed of separately.

Know this—nothing GREAT, nothing TRANSFORMATIVE, nothing that ever shaped the COMMON GOOD and INSPIRED others has ever happened except by thinking big.

Alice Coles of Bayview, Virginia, thought big and saved her community. In the late 1990s, Bayview was isolated and forgotten. The residents lived in the kind of poverty most Americans think exists only somewhere far away. Despite the squalor, it was a tightly knit community, founded on a proud history of settlers from among the slaves freed after the Civil War. Then the State of Virginia decided to build a maximum-security prison right in the middle of the community. Alice Coles, a 45-year-old single mother of two children, with nothing more than a high school education, making $5,000 a year crab picking, said "No." She wasn't someone with the kind of power or resources to get what she wanted. But she did. She organized the Bayview Citizens for Social Justice, which cleaned up the community and secured government money to revitalize the community. Much better than killing it with a prison. Alice Coles, together with others, helped to make the lives of everyone in Bayview better and more productive. That's thinking big.

Alice Coles thought big about her community and did the right thing.

Thinking big means transcending our small thoughts. *I'm not smart enough; I can't risk my secure job on some flimflam dream; my parents [spouse, children, friends] won't approve; people will think I'm crazy; nobody will like me anymore; I don't have the time; I don't have the energy; I can't make a difference, I'm only one person; I don't . . .; I can't . . .*

When we think like that, we are wrong, just plain wrong. We are thinking small. We are letting ourselves be diminished by other people's lack of imagination or our own impoverished imagination. We are succumbing to the mind-numbing small thoughts that our society favors. Why live my life when I can watch reality TV instead?

Small thoughts are not reality (nor, for that matter, is what's on television). You are more than you think. You can do more with your own life and you can have an impact on the larger world outside yourself—your family, your community, your country, our global village. The society we live in (televised, advertised, media-saturated, politically compromised, and corporate-controlled) does not have to be the way it is. It is not the only possibility. We can change things, starting with ourselves. Together.

We are the biggest obstacle that stands in the way of our doing big things in the world. We are our own worst enemies. Do you want to think bigger about who you are and what you offer the world? I know I do. We all do. Are you hesitating, not sure whether you want to think big? It's terrifying to let people in on our hopes and dreams. Sarcasm and irony can feel so much safer. It's called a _comfort zone_ for a reason—it's comfortable. But believe me, it's not worth it to pretend to have no important aspirations, because we are too fearful of being laughed at, or failing, or generally getting outside our comfort zone, so instead we say we don't want success. Do you want to succeed? I believe in you. I believe that you can think bigger about who you are and what you offer the world. Go ahead. Thinking big is easy . . . well, and hard, too. The easy part is—just do it. Think big. The hard part is dealing every day with our own small thoughts and those of others that threaten to sabotage our self-confidence. This is where the buck stops. This is our manifesto after all. We the people will think bigger about who we are and what we offer the world.

GURU-FREE ZONE

You've probably noticed that I use the words _we_ and _our_ a lot, as in _our_ manifesto. Sure, I am technically the author of this manifesto; someone had to write it. But don't mistake me for a guru. For one thing, I am no guru. For another thing, I have never met a real guru, and neither have you. "Guru-izing" people is a classic example of small thinking. In fact, we spend so much time guru-izing people that we have fallen into the guru trap. It is a trap that distorts our view of ourselves by fooling us into believing that we are somehow different (i.e., lesser) than the guru. That gurus are special, blessed—*something*—and that's why they can do big things in the world (and why we can't). We think gurus can do no wrong, that they have all the answers. What nonsense.

No one has all the answers. Maybe it's comforting to imagine that some guru knows all. In fact, we are, all of us, surprisingly similar on the inside. Now is a good time to escape the guru trap. The answers we are looking for are inside us. Together, we're going to explore the questions.

You will not find in these pages any immediate, guru-style 1-2-3 answers. Nor will you find the easy incremental solution: "Oh, it's okay if you don't do it all the way, halfway is fine." No, it's not. Thinking big is about a complete, a radical commitment to change—without a guru to hold your hand. Imagine that. There are no gurus here, just you and me and the big community we're building; and we're better than any guru any day.

THIS THINKING BIG THING COULD BE SCARY ...

Scary? Why? Because the small thinking powers-that-be do not want us to think big—and they definitely do not want us to act on our big thoughts. They want us to be tame and predictable, hooked up to the IV of television and shopping, living in our comfortable-life comas. Life is so much easier that way. The *citizens* (that means us) are tame. The corporations and politicians do what they want. The few can control the many. Is that what you want?

Of course not. Besides, if you're reading this book, you have no choice. You are already awake to the contagious, catalytic power of big thinking. You are ready to look inward and outward, to think bigger about who you are and what you offer the world.

I, for one, have pledged to fight consciously every day against the small thoughts that threaten to derail my plans, my aspirations, and my dreams. Sure, I still have them. I'm just like you and you are like me. We are in this thinking big business as a team.

> We pledge to FIGHT CONSCIOUSLY every day against the small thoughts that threaten to derail our plans, our ASPIRATIONS, and our DREAMS.

Here's a small example of big versus small thinking from my life. When I first started acting, I thought big. (Yes, I started my professional life as an actor and had a modicum of success. You can look me up on IMDB.com to see what I was in.) I didn't think, "Why me?" That's the kind of thinking that keeps you down. I thought, "Why *not* me?" That's the kind of thinking that can get you places. It got me into NYU's Graduate Acting Program, one of only 18 accepted from more than a thousand applicants.

Then the day-in, day-out grind of acting for a living started to wear me down. I let small thoughts seep in: *There are no good roles. I'll never make it. How much longer? Who are these idiots deciding who works and who doesn't?* I was losing the battle with my small thoughts, even though I was successful by most conventional measures. The other problem was that I just didn't like the lifestyle anymore—the uncertainty of when an audition might come up and then waiting for the result. I needed to get back to the big thinking that got me into acting school and get my life on course to where I wanted it to be.

I decided I should go into something more oriented toward marketing and business. I decided I had a head for it. Based on what? Based on thinking big again. I didn't have a business background, and both my parents are in the headshrinking business. I just believed it was something I could do. I was right and lucky (but would you really call it luck?). Thinking big and changing the direction of my life was a risk that's paid me dividends in happiness and fulfillment.

Thinking big is a massive endeavor. What that actually means for each of us is different. You will think big on your individual, radical scale, a scale that will change as you change. Effort is not absolute. One person's challenge is another's piece of cake and (this is the important thing to remember) vice versa.

For one person, doing a one-mile run may be as easy as breathing; for another, it may be a personal mountain to climb. Reverse the roles and the easy-breathing milers may find the idea of leaving their dead-end jobs terrifying to even contemplate, whereas the aspiring milers may be risk-taking entrepreneurs. When you are thinking big, you will be climbing your mountains. And the more peaks you climb, the taller they will become.

One mile becomes two, three, and then ten miles. Leaving a dead-end job becomes asking for a promotion at your next job, asking again, and building a career. Then it becomes about inspiring others to take on their challenges. By changing our own life for the better, in the process we change others' lives. The effect multiplies. The world changes.

Should you think big every day? Yes. Do I? No. I want to. And I try. By reading this book, you challenge me to work harder to think big every day. I'm up for it. Are you?

This is not a book for the fainthearted, but then neither is thinking big. I'm going to invite you to put yourself out there, to admit publicly your goals and ambitions, and, yes, to risk failure. Making a quantum change takes courage. It takes vision. There's no "Oh, well, maybe a little bit, yikes, maybe not." To transform yourself into someone who thinks big, you have to be 100 percent committed.

You'll see—thinking big is worth every ounce of effort, because once you start thinking big it takes you more places than you dreamed of. And to help you dream of more, in these pages you'll find stories from the inspiring and amazing people I've had the privilege to encounter in my personal and professional life, as well as so many of the members of the Think Big Revolution. If you've read my other books, you may recognize a few of the people, but there are so many more here, and, of course, the community of big thinkers is growing at ThinkBigRevolution. com. Don't wait to finish the book to join or start a revolution. That's part of thinking big. You won't have all the answers in advance, and you certainly won't have them all when you finish this manifesto.

WHAT WILL IT ALL ADD UP TO?

All this has been a bit general: Think big; commit to quantum change; envision your future; climb your mountains. By now you're probably wondering how it can actually transform your day-to-day life. The first answer is, I don't know. I warned you I didn't have answers. For everyone the outcome of thinking big will be different. That said, here's a short list of the kinds of practical things you may do when you start to think big:

- Build your own business
- Ask for (and get) a promotion
- Change jobs

- Change careers
- Get married
- Find the love of your life
- Come out of the closet
- Lose weight
- Leave an unhealthy relationship
- Adopt a child
- Start a charitable organization
- Volunteer for a nonprofit
- Green your home
- Start a farmers' market
- Learn how to cook
- Open a restaurant
- Go back to school
- Get involved with politics
- Save the whales
- Invent that *thing* you've been thinking about for years
- Take up painting
- Audition for a role in your local theater company
- Invest in real estate

- Start exercising
- Do a marathon
- Eat healthier
- Meditate
- Be fulfilled
- Be happy
- Be happier

In my case, this book is what happened when I started thinking big. I have wanted to write this book for a long time, but the personal scale was wrong for me to start with it. First I had other mountains to climb, maybe smaller and less ambitious. I wrote three other books. They were safer books, on socially acceptable topics (at least in my social circle), but each one brought me closer to this one. My books are successful in their field, yet there was always the idea for this manifesto, a book that reached higher, that wanted a bigger audience, that aspired to change the world. Can you believe I said that in black and white, here, in the book itself? Just as I'm going to suggest you do, I'm making public my big thoughts and aspirations.

I am thinking big about this book, and my profound hope is that I'll inspire you and many, many others to think big with me.

This is a manifesto, after all; and a manifesto's purpose is to galvanize, to catalyze, and to energize. To do this properly, we need to begin the next section with the essential of every manifesto—its statement of purpose.

III.
STATEMENT OF THE THINK BIG REVOLUTION

RISE UP

The time has come. We cannot wait anymore. For years we have hidden behind our own small thoughts or let ourselves be held back by other small thinking people who don't believe in us. Worse still, we have been rejected as marginal, unrealistic, dreamers, idealists, maybe even delusional. Family, friends, colleagues, and others (not to mention our own selves) have tried to negate us, eliminate us, and silence us. We will not stand for it anymore. We say—bring it on. Our personal revolution from small thinking to big thinking is now. We will make public our aim to think big about our goals, our intentions, and, yes, our dreams.

There's more. We will collaborate, cooperate, and join forces with other big thinkers to bring about the larger revolution our society needs if it is to survive.

You want to think big. I want to think big. Together, we will think even bigger.

I can almost hear some of you thinking—did he really say *rise up*? Isn't *survive* a bit strong? Well . . . actually, yes and no. This is a revolution we're talking about here, and if you think survive is a bit "too, too," read the news more often—other than the latest on Brangelina. There's a war on. There's some heavy environmental stress that's coming to a boil, so to speak. There's too much poverty. There's not enough health care. There are children who can't read. I could go on. This is a manifesto, no sugarcoating. Our personal aspirations are part of a bigger picture. If we are to think big about ourselves, we need to understand this world we live in and how we want to be in it.

Okay. Rewind. Rise up. Fast-forward. Roll again.

WHO ARE WE?

We is me and you . . . and we are people who are thinking bigger about who we are and what we offer the world. We are people who believe in working together with others to do big things, instead of isolating ourselves in competition against others. We are big thinkers.

WHO AND WHAT ARE WE UP AGAINST?

We are up against a society controlled by people and institutions who generally think small. The corporation that seeks to control and manipulate what you think, what you buy, what you believe; the friend who tells you not to be too big for your britches; the husband who dominates his wife and makes her feel irrelevant; the teacher who tells you there is only one way to do something; the television networks who want to dumb you down; the news media who want to tell you lies and answer no questions; the self-help guru who has a blueprint that will fix you, but only if you invest your life savings in a secret program.

I can't fix you; not only that, you're not even broken !

We will be ridiculed for declaring ourselves to be big thinkers. To declare anything is to take a chance, to put ourselves on the line, to risk failure. I did it earlier, remember? I told you my hopes and dreams for this book. I might fail. Failure is nothing. It will happen. We will transcend it.

When we take risks we scare other people (and most of all ourselves), because those others see the glimmer of possibilities that they are not even reaching for, because the potential of our success makes them face their own universe, so constricted by their small thoughts.

Know that we reach **only what we aim for, so there is no choice but to aim** high **if we are to** succeed **.**

We will be put down for our efforts. Others will revel in our failures along the way. In the German language, there's even a word for it: *schadenfreude*. To feel pleasure at someone else's misfortune. Small, small thinking.

We may lose faith in ourselves at points along the way. Worse, we will be intentionally thwarted by small thinking people who fear big thinking because it threatens their comfortable power base.

Together we will find our warrior core, our inner strength, the root of big thinking, and nothing and no one can thwart us.

THE THINK BIG REVOLUTION

Understand two things:

(1.) Powerful new ideas, big ideas, have always been met with suspicion and fear, from our nearest and dearest to the unknown many. This fear only confirms that we will succeed.

(2.) We are overdue. It is past time for us to start thinking big about who we are and what we offer the
world. Now we will be open about our ambitions
and aspirations. We will meet the small thinking and fearmongering perpetuated by those in
power with this, our manifesto.

Every big thinker and potential big thinker (which is basi-
cally everyone), will use this as their guide, their road
map, and their catalyst to start their own personal revolution and come together in the larger revolution that will,
as a matter of course, result from our combined efforts.

This is a revolution that will eradicate small thoughts
from our lexicon (our vocabulary and our internal
dictionary) . . . a revolution that will remove small thinking people from their positions of influence . . . a revolution that will change the way society is structured, what
it values, and who is in power.

Thinking big will produce a society that prizes people of
values, not people who have net value; that elects people
of principles, not people with cronies who have the most
principal in their bank accounts; that seeks truth, not
trite, media-generated baby food to distract us from the
realities of our world; that considers that each and every
one of us has the potential to think big about ourselves.

IV.

THE CASE FOR

BIG THINKING

(OR THE CASE AGAINST SMALL THINKING)

Consumer warning: These next few pages may seem negative. But there's a reason. Even if we know we want to think big, we still may be having trouble. So what? Does it really matter if we keep thinking small? What are my dreams to the world? It matters.

Your dreams matter to the world.

Thinking small is no longer an alternative. Fatalistic thinking has never worked. It's killing us—our society, our environment, our dreams. I think we need to deal with it. We live in the world. We need to understand it. More—our world needs us. Sometimes thinking big means facing up to some harsh realities, like the cost of thinking small. Here goes. Let's start with a few reminders. It might not be pretty.

Throughout history, small thoughts have stood in opposition to big thoughts. The church reviled Galileo. The earth is flat, right? Darwin was disbelieved in his time. We couldn't possibly be descended from apes, could we? Slave owners fought to the death to prevent abolition. Men did not let women vote. Jazz was deemed illicit. Someone tried to kill the electric car. Books (and sometimes even the publishers' offices) continue to be burned. Writers are incarcerated. We are poisoning our environment, but no one wants to take personal responsibility for their treatment of our planet and so we keep on guzzling gas, consuming stuff, stuff, and more stuff and piling up trash. Endless wars are waged because nobody wants to let go of their hatred and moral posturing long enough to enable peace.

Albert Einstein once said, "Great spirits have always found violent opposition from mediocrities. The latter cannot understand it when a man does not thoughtlessly submit to hereditary prejudices, but honestly and courageously uses his intelligence and fulfills the duty to express the results of his thought in clear form."

THINKING SMALL VERSUS THINKING BIG

People dominated by their small thoughts and those who are thinking big struggle against one another: the fully self-expressed artists versus those in self-imposed I-can't-be/do boxes; the bold entrepreneurs versus those who dare not dream; the blissfully happy lovers versus those who deny their vulnerability and thus their capacity to love; those who live large versus those who live in ministorage; the adventurers eager to explore new territory, new ideas, and new ways of being versus those set in their ways, whether by rigidity or timidity; those who choose abundance versus those who choose scarcity; those who do today what they could do tomorrow versus those who plan to plan; those who seek answers versus those who think they have all the answers; those who say "we" versus those who say "them," thereby creating a separation between *me* and *others* makes *we* exclusive instead of inclusive.

We are in crisis. We live in a time when the individual and the corporation have merged almost seamlessly. We can hardly distinguish what any individual thinks versus what we are told to think by corporations, by the media, and by the government, all of whom want to control us, whether it is to dictate what we buy or what we believe. Small thinking.

We will **not** be **controlled**.

In this age of abundance, gluttonous excess even, when the world is flatter every day, more economically networked, and globalized to the nth degree, hostility toward big thinkers' spiritual, emotional, and intellectual beliefs is at an all-time high. Monopoly-controlled print, broadcast, and streaming media; consumerism;

fundamentalism and other religious extremism—all of these place power in the hands of people thinking too, too small, meaning dogmatic teachers, self-interested politicians, profit-at-all-costs businesses, self-appointed gurus, and others whose interests neglect the well-being of the largest portions of society, often including their own interests. *Including their own interests*—try to imagine—it defies reason. Why would people act with intent against their own interests? Yet we do. Freud had a theory about it—the *death drive*, which he thought was an innate, biological resistance that people have against bettering themselves. He's been proved wrong before. We'll prove him wrong again.

THINKING SMALL

The power base in our country is dominated by small thinking, and those in control strive to build and perpetuate a domestic and international culture of more and more sedated citizens (*read* me and you). They want us to think small so that we will willingly act against our own interests and the interests of our children and generations to come. Why else would the poor be getting poorer and the rich richer? Why else would the environment be going to the dogs and war be slipping into the indefinite state of being?

The sheer volume and extraordinary decibel level of small thinking can drown out the best-intentioned entrepreneurial fervor, creative enthusiasm, racial harmony, environmental conservation, political progress, and true human values in the icy water of egotistical, self-interested, hypercommercial calculation.

We will not be drowned out.

Our small thinking society has resolved personal worth into a solely transactional value: "The Donald Trump Pseudo-Big Way." *How much do you make? What things do you own? Who have you conquered along the way?* The small thinking path to success is littered with the carcasses of others who have been stepped on and over.

For the record, Mr. Trump: Thinking big never belongs in the same sentence as kicking ass. Never. Thinking big is not now and never will be the same thing as taking advantage of others (i.e., kicking ass). Trump is hardly the only one. Enron's higher-ups seemed to be thinking big, but then it turned out they were just really good at taking advantage of other people, at least for a while. I'm sure you can think of other even more recent examples.

You will never see big thinkers winning at someone else's expense or taking more than their fair share. (Should *any* CEOs make more than 30,000 times what one of their employees makes?)

In place of the internationally chartered civil, political, social, and economic rights and freedoms, which incidentally also coincide with just about every secular and nonsecular moral code, small thinking has set up a single, unconscionable unfreedom—*fate*, propagating and perpetuating the idea that you can't change your present or your future, that everything is preordained, and no one cares, anyway, as long as there's lots of *stuff.* Note, too, that not everyone is as glutted with stuff as we are here in the West. Yet we seem to forget our luck in our pursuit of more, more, more.

Think: "Why not me?" instead of "Why me?"

My friend Jeremy was a supersuccessful hedge fund manager. He once said to me, "I figured there was all this money out there, why shouldn't I pick some of it up?" That's thinking big, saying, "Why not me?" instead of "Why me?" And Jeremy did pick up quite a bit of the money out there. Jeremy would never say that money wasn't important, nor would I. He likes his *stuff*. I do, too. But that's not the same thing as valuing stuff above all else; and that's not the same thing as being sedated by our stuff. For Jeremy, money was a tool, not the end goal. And there came a point when Jeremy realized that just making money was not fulfilling, so he thought even bigger. He stepped off the money train, the stuff-accumulation train, to live his life in a whole new way. Now he's an organic cattle farmer and happy as pig in . . . you know what. He spends time with his family. He spends time outdoors. And he can dream up new philanthropic ways to give back. Nothing about Jeremy's life was preordained, and he didn't let stuff lull him into small thinking. Too many give in to what they think is their fate, soothed by their relative economic comfort into thinking it's all they can have or deserve.

If right now you're thinking, "It's easy for him to think big, he's rich," stop. Number one—he didn't make money by accident. He did it because he was thinking big. I've said this book is not about making money, and it's not. There are so many other things that we might value as an end goal. But if making money is your end goal, then one of the surest ways to get there is by thinking big. Number two—far too many who do make money are not thinking big and don't give back. Those who do, like Jeremy, are proof, if it were needed, that making money does not necessarily corrupt big thinking.

Universal aspirations have been replaced by universal illusions. Truth, and the search for all but the most facile, meaningless meaning, has been replaced by the desire for ease and comfort and permission not to think for oneself. How has this happened? Why do we allow it? The ways in which big thinking is suppressed are many, and everyone who thinks big has encountered a host of barricades and disincentives to thinking big.

Here are five of the most pernicious, insidious small thoughts that keep us from thinking big and maintain the illusion that small thinking is right thinking.

(1.) The small idea that what we've received from our past determines what's in store for our future

(2.) The small idea that who we are and what we have today is not enough (will never be enough) and is shameful

(3.) The small idea that winning requires a loser

(4.) The small idea that we can expect of our future nothing more than the most diminished, pessimistic, negative, hopeless version of reality to come

(5.) The small idea that being *realistic* or *practical*
    means settling for less

No one is free from small thoughts and their subversive
nature. Small thoughts subversively strip away the fire
of imagination, the generosity of the collaborative spirit,
and the halo of every dream. Small thoughts convert the
mother, the physician, the lawyer, the priest, the poet,
the scientist, and the politician from people striving
to the highest personal standard into interchangeable
pod people for whom being like everyone else is the
most important thing.

When we think small, we abuse our natural desire for
(and inherent right to) abundance. Corporations were
once thought to be benevolent patrons of commerce and
society at large. If that quaint notion were ever true, which
many now doubt, that sentimental veil has most certainly
been torn away. Brutal displays of corporate greed are
matched only by our small thinking passivity. Corporate,
religious, government, and media promises of the Garden
of Eden are received and believed without question
with the most slothful intellectual, political, physical, and
emotional indolence imaginable.

Sure, sometimes small thoughts disguise old wine in
new bottles. Everyone loves shiny things; I certainly do,

but that's no guarantee of anything except shininess (not to mention that shiny things become dull over time). Small thinking perpetuates the past and encourages the false notion that we can never rid ourselves of any of the excess baggage we carry from the past, our long-held prejudices and opinions.

It is never too late to ABANDON our PREJUDICES, to rethink, to THINK deeply again, again, and again about the world and what is RIGHT.

Small thinking has exploited the flat world, the virtually interconnected world, and globalization to give character and significance to the consumption of mind-numbing, irrelevant, low-vibration pop culture in every country and to the creation of a disposable society of throwaway goods, throwaway people, and throwaway dreams.

The least glimmer of a distant hope or dream sinks into the sludge of small thinking. Maybe I will go for that walk today. Maybe I won't eat at McDonald's today. On second thought, it is a lot easier to take a pill for my health than to worry about self-discipline.

Where once small thoughts were private and self-sufficient, they were also, of course, self-destructive; as our interconnectedness increases, and we now connect in every direction, a universal interdependence has been created, and small thoughts are propagated farther and wider and deeper. We become the instruments of our own small thoughts, and the larger community of people thinking small likewise propagates a kind of wiki-small-thinking process of assimilation and groupthink. Even when we are capable of big thinking in the right environment (and almost all of us are), instead we let ourselves be crushed under the contagious weight of small thinking.

New big thoughts, habits, and creative concepts are becoming more and more impossible; and through the increasing number of small thinking, international, national, and local media distribution channels, a small thinking, anti-intellectual world literature, world philosophy, and world economy is developing—*a world anesthesia.*

The cheap price of small thoughts—the ease with which they can be swallowed whole, no muss, no fuss, no work, no effort—breaks down the obstinate resistance of our bold, big thoughts. We are struggling to hang onto our goals, ideas, ideals, and dreams. Small thoughts make it too easy to capitulate and too difficult to resist. Small thinking prevents new ideas from flourishing, stops true innovations, and discourages direct and intentional actions toward our dreams. Small thinking compels us, on pain of extinction (because who wants to be the only big thinker—a weirdo, a freak?), to adopt the small thinking mode of existence. So-called progress in our society is big thoughts making way for small thoughts.

Small thinking creates a world after its own image, a world of ever-smaller thinkers, safe only after all its drones are hooked forever on the mutual life support system of small thoughts.

We worship greed and self-centeredness. The extreme disparity of wealth, of access to opportunity, goes largely unnoticed. When Hurricane Katrina hit New Orleans, people were galvanized by the breadth of the tragedy, but New Orleans, and in particular the Ninth Ward, was already in crisis—a crisis of poverty, of lack of social services, of lack of the basic necessities that most Americans expect as routine. Why weren't people galvanized by that prior crisis? Because they didn't know it existed. Because they didn't believe it could exist in their country.

We have been sleeping through our lives. We have been lulled into thinking everything is okay. Consequently, when we want to think bigger, we lose our motivation and drive. To achieve even the barest first step of any big thought requires almost more energy than it generates. Note that I said _almost_.

The truth is that big thinking is always, always [always, always, always] worth the expenditure of energy.

Yet the cost of small thinking has skyrocketed. With small thinking, we cannot grow—intellectually, spiritually, creatively, emotionally, financially. And when we cannot grow, society cannot grow. It cannot advance. It cannot develop. Small thinking is an ultimately autodestructive path. The cost of small thoughts will increase geometrically until it exceeds society's ability to pay. What's more—the modern small thought support system (television, glossy magazines with surreal photos of the *perfect* life, political and corporate indecency, religious extremism, etc.) only increases the speed and effectiveness of the spread of small thoughts.

We become slaves to small thoughts. We live in the thrall of the new big brother. We are the puppets of the gremlin on our shoulder, telling us what we can't do, can't strive for, can't even dream. Instead, we are fed the message that the accumulation of wealth and possessions is the only true end, and the more the message is absorbed, the more it sinks into the marrow of our being, the pettier, the more hateful, and the more embittering it is.

....

The only reward of SMALL THINKING will be paid in the common currency of all small thinking—UNACCOMPLISHED DREAMS.

....

What have we become?

No growth—not spiritual, emotional, professional, or social—is possible in this kind of environment.

We are squandering the gifts of the universe.

THINKING BIG

And yet . . . and yet . . . there is hope—think big. With and within those of us who are willing to think big lies the potential for growth, the wellspring of renewal. Growth springs from the broad, expansive, big thinking of a conscious mind and soul. Better still—there is no either-or about it. Even if we've been thinking small, we need not continue to do so. We can all think big. There is more than enough room in the world for everyone to grow.

We have within our grasp the potential for a society of fully self-expressed big thinking people. If only we will first face head-on the real condition of our life, our relationships, and our beliefs and own up to our complicity in perpetuating our own small thoughts and those of others. At the same time, to gain a foothold, airspace, eyeballs, and influence, we must establish actual and virtual connections between those of us who are thinking big everywhere around the world. Together we can, we will, and we must join, participate in, and lead the Think Big Revolution.

Become the kind of person who lives best when you express yourself and who accomplishes bigger and bigger goals by collaborating with others. Strive always toward full self-expression. Then you will be a catalyst for change. It's hard, very hard.

> Remember this: Small thinking always says "No, no." It's up to YOU and ME to say "YES, yes."

To think big is to embark on a path of development, a series of personal revolutions, an intellectual awakening, a process of opening up to the world around you, the exchange of ideas, and the flow of energy when people truly work together. At every step along the way you will experience your own political, social, moral, financial, ethical, and spiritual advancement and the advancement of others around you. Just as others who have thought big throughout history, you can and will play a revolutionary role in the development of your community, family, government, economy, and the institutions you are connected with.

Put an end to destructive, manipulative, parasitic, oppressive relationships. Cut loose the ties that pretend to bind people to their supposed superiors, to their gurus, to their politicians, to their religious advisers, and to their teachers; instead, build a new web of connections between people based on collaboration, service, meaning, and, yes, even (and above all) love.

What will we face?

We are the first step in the Think Big Revolution. The first step in the struggle between big thoughts and small thoughts is the personal challenge each one of us will face.

There are stages in the development of most big thinking. Few of us are able to totally withstand the pressures of small thinking exerted on us in childhood and early adulthood. From the start, you have probably struggled against a barrage of small thoughts, consciously or unconsciously. Now make the struggle conscious.

Once conscious of your intent to think big, you will find the others like you—like me and this manifesto. It's like a secret handshake, only there's nothing hidden about it. The absolute hallmark of big thinking is its wide-open abundance. Collaborations between you and others will start happening, the beginning of a revolution. This in turn will spread to a broader community. We're out here—waiting for you to join us.

We're already consciously thinking big, working together to improve our lots and the lives of others. As the word spreads, we will inevitably be drawn together. There is a gravitational pull among big thoughts that grows stronger as our numbers increase. As each collaborative effort bears fruit, it will inspire yet more.

As you band together with others who are thinking big, you will be faced with a similarly growing pressure of small thinking that threatens to deprive you of your inspiration and accomplishments.

What do you fear? What is your future?

Other people's small thoughts are not your enemy. Direct your struggle ever inward against your own small thoughts. Turn away from, tune out, and unplug the small thoughts that sneak in. All those *I-can't-I-don't* thoughts have no place. Set the tired dogma of those small thoughts ablaze with the kerosene strength of your curiosity and creativity. Restore openness with your passion. You will find that you are more and more in tune with others—and even, I'll go ahead and say it, with the universe.

Did you just think, "There he goes again?" A moment ago, in that last paragraph, I was almost embarrassed to write about becoming more in tune with the universe. Why? Because it sounds hokey? Yes, but the *why* of my hesitation was because I struggle with small thoughts on a daily basis. That moment was one such moment. While I was writing the words, I thought that others (not me) would find it implausible and then I would be discredited. I thought I ought to be more cautious, hold back what I truly think to make it more palatable. In the end, I didn't. The words are there. The *I-can't-write-that* thought did not win out. No matter how big you think, you will likely continue to struggle (maybe even daily) not only against the small thoughts of others, but more important, against your own small thoughts. I haven't given up yet. Don't you give up. We're in this together. We don't have to agree on everything to do big things together or to stand side by side.

As with all revolutions, as the Think Big Revolution grows larger in numbers and we feel the weight of our big ideas gaining density, we will be galvanized. So, too, at first, will the small thinking masses, anxious to protect their numbed security.

Do not let your imagination fail. Nothing happens in an instant. There are no easy victories, only important ones. Stay the course. It could be years until we achieve the ultimate goals we set out to achieve. Yet in the interim, nothing is lost. Every day that we live resolved to think bigger about who we are and what we offer the world is its own personal victory.

Daniel Dae Kim stretched his imagination. Here's the story of his personal victory: Dan and I attended the Graduate Acting Program at NYU's Tisch School of the Arts together and became good friends. He's a talented actor. But . . . he's an Asian-American man. So when we got out of school he was getting only the usual secondary roles that Asian men get—you know, the forensic doctor, the lab technician—never the sex symbol or the leading role. Sure, he did some cool theater, Off-Off-Broadway. But he's a bright guy. He had options. So he left acting and worked for a couple of years at a dot-com. He is a husband and father of two beautiful boys. That should have been the end of his acting career. The prevailing wisdom is that you can't come back to acting after an absence unless you were a big star before you left. The prevailing wisdom is that once you have a wife and family, your risk-taking days are over and you better just stay put in your pay-the-bills job. Well, Dan thought big. He decided that not only was he going back to acting, he was going to get parts that were not typically given to Asian men. It was that determination and big thinking that enabled him to capture a leading role on the television show *LOST.* Now he's a star and a sex symbol, to boot. Not that being a sex symbol is important to Dan, but he's paving the way for future generations of Asian-American actors and changing the way Americans see Asian-American men. And that is important to him. The only thing holding you back from taking the risks you need to succeed at what you want is your own small thinking.

Not all of us want to be television stars. What we think big about is up to us. It's our personal revolution, remember? Maybe you bought a hybrid car. Maybe you marched for peace. Maybe you quit the job you hated, but you haven't found the one you love yet. Maybe you got the twenty-first rejection on a book you've written, but you still know it's a good book. What if J. K. Rowling, a struggling single mother, had given up? Maybe you haven't written the next *Harry Potter*, but maybe you have. You are not giving up. Even if your hybrid car seems like a drop in the bucket, your march fruitless, and your economic situation less secure than it once was, you will not give up and give in to the small thoughts trying hard to ride you into the ground.

Sometimes we will feel ourselves drawn into competition with others who are thinking big. That's natural. Unlike the entropy of small thinking, which competition forces to the lowest common denominator in a downward spiral, true big thinking transforms competition into cooperation, which only strengthens the overall results. Collaborating accomplishes so much more than the individual isolation of most competition.

In case you were wondering, that word *entropy* that I used just now is dictionary-defined as "measure of the degradation or disorganization of the universe." It is too apt a term not to use. If small thinking = entropy, disorganization, and degradation, then big thinking = blossoming, growth, and love.

THE REVOLUTION

Virtually all previous historical revolutionary movements were movements of minorities, or temporary coalitions of minorities who, once the early struggle was complete, turned on each other. The Think Big Revolution is a self-conscious, independent movement operating in the interest of the immense majority. In fact, even those individuals who, wedded to their small thinking ways, may feel threatened by big thinking will soon find that they, too, will benefit.

This is a one-way revolution. It gives to everyone and takes away from no one.

This is not a revolt of *us* against *them*. In the end there will be no *them*, only *we*. This is each of us seizing the opportunity for self-empowerment. Sure, there may be some loss of power by those thinking small, but in the end, it will be clear that it was fear they lost, not power.

Until now, almost every form of society has been based on some version of the antagonism between powerful and powerless. Society cannot function properly in this condition of perpetual repression. No form of repressive existence is compatible with a big thinking society. True big thinking, like true democracy, is a society of equals, a level playing field the likes of which we've never seen before. The majority does not oppress a minority. Nor does a privileged minority disenfranchise a less privileged majority. Equal opportunity does not mean that everyone is identical, far from it. It does mean that each and every one of us has the freedom, responsibility, and capacity to think bigger about who we are and what we have to offer the world.

As a founding principle, the Think Big Revolution requires the formation and augmentation of intellectual and spiritual capital.

> The condition for INTELLECTUAL capital is big thoughts. The condition for SPIRITUAL capital is love. The future of big thinking rests exclusively on the COMBINATION of both.

The advancement of and growth of intellectual capital through study and learning in action with others will replace the isolation of small thinking. This revolutionary combination will cut loose the very foundation on which the old-school small thoughts were generated and propagated. In place of small thoughts and small thinking, we will have big thoughts and big thinking, fully self-expressed, self-actualized, collaborative contributors to society, who know no limitations and no limits. After all, that's what love is, too.

V.

THE CODE
(JOIN THE REVOLUTION
IN PROGRESS, OR
START YOUR OWN)

How will we do it? It's easy. Sit in a comfortable chair and think really hard until big thoughts come. Okay, it's not that easy. In fact, I can't give you a simple 1-2-3, the five rules to follow, or the 12 steps. Thinking big is more like breathing—complicated and simple. Like breathing, it ought to come naturally, and probably would, if it weren't for all the social conditioning that we're exposed to as we're growing up. Like breathing, too, when you try to break it down into its component pieces it can seem pretty complex.

Annie Leonard, the big thinking filmmaker responsible for the surprise Internet phenomenon, *The Story of Stuff,* by turns a hilarious and chilling 20-minute film that takes viewers on a provocative and eye-opening tour of the real costs of our consumer driven culture, from resource extraction to iPod incineration, is often asked for a list of simple steps that will help people to get involved. For a couple of reasons, she intentionally will not provide specific recommendations for action. Real solutions don't lend themselves to sound bites, and she does not want to prescribe and limit the actions each viewer may choose to do. Annie refuses to simplify what's complicated. We should be glad of this. At last, someone who is not spoon-feeding us. If we really want to change things, we must be prepared and willing to spend time finding real, long-term solutions. We need to spend the time it takes to think big.

Thinking big may not be as easy as 1-2-3, but it is natural, once you get used to it. As such, it follows a natural order, what we might call a *code*. This code consists of the unwavering principles, the new standards, the values that every big thinker adheres to. To live by these principles, to rise to these standards, to adhere to this code is to think big. To be guided by this code is to reject the norms of small thinking, the old standards that hold us back, that keep us from our hopes and dreams. It is living by these principles, through which you will discover the code of conduct for thinking big and through which you will unleash the power of your creativity, the flame of your passion, the potential of your life, and, I'll say it again, love. From love comes life force. To paraphrase one of the training principles of the inimitable Bruce Lee, without love for each other, we are nothing but barbarians.

> Thinking big is a REVOLUTION, not a process. The code is not a blueprint. It is a call to immediate ACTION. It is the way in which you will think BIG in every aspect of your LIFE.

Because thinking big is natural, I wanted to find a way to introduce you to its code, its principles, and its standards that reflect this. In thinking about how we discover and define what is natural in the world, I encountered Fibonacci numbers, a sequence that describes much of beauty in the world. Think of the sunflower, that bright smile of flowers: The ratio of inside and outside petals follows a Fibonacci sequence. Think, too, of the chambered seashell, the nautilus, that we love to hold to our ear to listen to the sound of the ocean, even when the ocean is hundreds of miles away. The shell grew by producing a series of ever-larger chambers. What's magical is that the proportions of each increasingly larger chamber are mathematically captured by the aesthetic sequence of the Fibonacci numbers.

The sequence goes like this: Each succeeding number is derived from the sum of the previous two. So it begins as 0, 1, 1, 2, 3, 5, 8 and so on.

Not only the nautilus, but much else follows this same elegant mathematical code, from the pinecone to the distribution of seeds in a plant. Beyond the realm of nature, Fibonacci sequencing has given form to music, to poetry, to geometric shapes, and to computer modeling. What seems to the senses to be simply the gorgeous variety of natural harmony is in fact subject to a code. So it is with thinking big.

To think big is a thing of beauty in keeping with the mathematical code of the Fibonacci numbers I have used its sequence to describe the principles of thinking big. I have another purpose in using this seemingly random numbering. That is, to demonstrate that no one of these principles has a higher priority than another. Rather, each builds on every other one, creating an interdependent web.

> There's NO right FIRST STEP and no last step. To begin to think big is ORGANIC. Once you start it will grow like the seashell, your thoughts EXPANDING ever upward and outward.

Unlike the Fibonacci sequence, there is no proper order to the principles in the pages that follow. You can dive in anywhere and read the principles of the code in any order. We can set aside the idea of sequencing and instead think of another powerful natural phenomenon— the spider's web, spun from silk stronger than anything we humans have so far been capable of producing. With these principles you will build a web of understanding and actions that will only strengthen each time you think big, and work with others to think bigger, until it is strong enough to withstand the inevitable small thoughts that will threaten to destabilize and undermine your big thinking. You may notice that similar ideas surface at changing angles, and in new contexts, as we weave the principles together to create our code, our own Think Big Revolution web.

You say you want a revolution? Keep reading.

0. STAND FOR SOMETHING (OR SOMEONE WILL STAND ON YOU)

The world is an abundant place.

Yet we think and act as if we are threatened by scarcity at every turn. Often we behave as though we are engaged in a zero-sum game, where for every winner there's necessarily a loser. Sure, there's some scarcity in the world. Some species are facing extinction (maybe even us if we're not more careful). We are told that oil and gas may be in short supply. But those aren't issues of scarcity. We have created these challenges. We can solve them. We can better protect endangered species, because *we* are the threat, not some unknown or unknowable. It's just a matter of changing our behavior. There is an abundance of solutions for improved fuel efficiency and alternative energy sources. We need only the will to act.

The only true scarcity in the world is our resistance to embracing our own true self, our hopes and dreams, our capacity to think big. We're all we've got, in the end. Resistance is futile (as they say). When we think small, we bury our true nature under fat layers of persona—professional, personal, Web-related, and other temporary disguises. We become a doctor because our mother or father was one, and though it is a worthy career, maybe it is not the one we would have chosen. Maybe I want to be a professional rock climber or a cellist. Maybe you want to be a sculptor or a translator. But no one supports us in this calling. Instead of following what our instinct, our spirit tells us, we follow what others tell us to do. By resisting ourselves, we create our own condition of scarcity.

What do you resist in yourself?

When we resist ourselves we create false scarcity: *I'm not enough. I'm not as good as . . . [pick a name]. It's too hard. There's no time. I can't start because I don't know how it will end.* When we focus on what we are not, what we do not have, and what we do not (and often cannot) know, we focus on a self-induced scarcity.

Each of us is naturally ABUNDANT. To exist is abundant. Look INSIDE and see the GLORY of who you are—more than good enough.

Instead, we look outside ourselves for the externally generated justification and gratification we think we need in order to matter, to be important, but that we can never fully get from someone else.

> We CANNOT (must not) WAIT for other people to tell us that we're WORTHWHILE.

I exist. You exist. We are. We are already important. We don't need someone else to tell us so. We have something to offer the world. We are the person we've been waiting for. As my friend and colleague, Kim George, author of *Coaching into Greatness,* says, "We are our own pot of gold at the end of the rainbow." We are the treasure we've been searching for. No one else can give us our true sense of self. That's why it's called *self.*

Thinking big is a journey inward to our essential nature, to our core. It is not a matter of adding things, of becoming something else, of being a different person. It is not a matter of finding *it.* Just the opposite. Thinking big is paring down, stripping away the excess. *It* is already there. It's you. It's me. Our core.

To think big is to begin by letting go of what we don't need—habits, attitudes, and beliefs that stand in the way of thinking big. "All that is not given is lost." That statement inspired Mike Berkley to follow his bliss. When he first heard it, he was a computer salesman. His sole justification for getting up in the morning was to see how many computers he could sell by the end of the day. While watching television one day, he happened upon a program about a woman, a saint in fact, who stood in the middle of a town taking off her clothes, piece by piece, and giving them away. Friends and passersby tried to stop her, thinking she was crazy, but she just said, "All that is not given is lost." Mike realized his life was about getting, not giving, and that was really just plain crazy. In one of those coincidences that happen when we're thinking big, Mike had a good friend, an acupuncturist, who had piqued Mike's interest in the field of acupuncture. A few days after seeing the saint on TV, Mike saw an ad for a new acupuncture school opening and he went to the open house. He stayed six years. Opened his own practice. Founded the Berkley Center for Reproductive Wellness and Women's Health, a chain of wellness centers that specialize in treating men's and women's infertility using acupuncture, herbal medicine, yoga, meditation, nutrition, and other modalities. Now he serves people every day. Mike Berkley stands for natural good health. He gives so as not to lose—himself.

Our CORE is that part of us that can NEVER be DESTROYED no matter what is done to us. We can be beaten and tortured, tormented by others. We can lose everything we own. We can lose the love of our life. But there is a part INSIDE of each of us that cannot be taken away. It is our core and it is RICH and ABUNDANT.

Nelson Mandela endured as much as any person can, and yet, after more than a quarter of a century behind bars, he emerged with a spirit of love and forgiveness. There could be no better model of the power of the core of a person to preserve its abundance, even in times of unimaginable scarcity. And that is what it means to think big. It is to understand that we need nothing except that which is inside each of us. We don't need more to do more. We can do more with less. The only thing we need is to know our core.

Thinking big is to be not the person prescribed by history, by society, or by the invisible panel of pseudopeers who contrive to rule through conformity. When you are thinking big, you simply are. You know the why of what you do. You walk the talk, always truthward-bound. To be truly revolutionary is to be radically transparent. You are a person turned inside out, your core rendered visible.

I'm not saying it's easy to know when you've whittled down enough to access your core. The core is an elusive entity. It is what we stand for. It is what we are about, what drives us to do what we do.

What do you wake up for in the morning? Does it fulfill you? Is it what you truly want to be doing?

Nor, once your core is identified, is it easy to expose it for the world to see. To let people know what we stand for is to lay ourselves bare, all those raw nerve endings reachable, touchable by others. It can make a person uncomfortable just to think about such vulnerability. Yet here's the paradox: To be so exposed is where our true strength resides. When we repress our dreams, thinking we have protected ourselves from getting hurt, from the power of others to adversely affect our lives, all we have really done is repress our dreams. We have wasted our resources on self-protection, and in the end it will never work. All that negative energy makes us weak. Our core is strong. Our core is founded on trust and truth and on love.

Thinking big is not and cannot be a rebellious act. It is an empowerment, not a revolt. It is not a response to something; it's not "I'm-going-to-show-them-just-watch-me-become . . . [fill in the blank]." To rebel is an action fueled by scarcity. A revolution is ultimately about creating something new, not simply revolting and rebelling against something in the past. To think big may begin with what seems like a rebellion against a status quo or a historical way of being, but it is so much more than that. If thinking big originates or ends with the revolt, with the act of tearing down what wasn't working, if it is simply one rebellious act after another, then we have been trapped by history rather than releasing ourselves from history.

To change our future, we cannot be prisoners of our past. Rebellion is simply acting out in the present against something in our past history. We must not allow ourselves to be trapped by our history. Yes, we are necessarily shaped by our pasts, and, yes, we must learn from history (why repeat mistakes?), but we are in control of our future. It's up to us to ensure that the past is not forcing us down a road not of our choosing. Frederick Banting, who won the 1923 Nobel Prize in Medicine for his invention of insulin, said in his later years that if he had been more familiar with the literature and the long history of unsuccessful attempts to isolate the extract that he did ultimately isolate (along with his collaborators, Best, MacLeod, and Collip, as no great work is done alone), then he might never have undertaken the research he did. Our capacity to do great things can never be measured by the past. The future is not bound by any precedents. As Randy Pausch writes in his book, *The Last Lecture*, "We cannot change the cards we are dealt, just how we play the hand." To think big is to choose our own destiny.

What things bind you to your past? Do you really need them, or are they holding you back?

To think big is an act of originality and creation, an act of abundance. It is finding that we already have the resources to do more, to make a better world. It is a willingness to express our ideals and ideas openly when necessary and the ability to listen to others. As Eleanor Roosevelt said, "The future belongs to those who believe in the beauty of their dreams." The closer to our core we travel, the more connected we are to what we stand for, the more energetic resources we will draw from the bottomless well of the human evolutionary reserves of self-trust and love. To live from our core is to stand for something, and that something is what is precious to each one of us.

You may be thinking—*but what if I'm not 100 percent sure what I stand for?* Or, *what if I feel like I stand for a whole lot of different things?* Of course, we all stand for lots of things, from racial equality to a more democratic access to education to animal rights—for truth, for reality, for kindness, for *something*. At our core, we stand for one thing. It is the fundamental principle that fuels us, that resonates in every fiber of our being. Frederick Banting stood for helping others in crisis, and he died in the service of what he stood for, while bandaging the wounds of a Canadian air force pilot headed to World War II, in a plane carrying both men that went down off Newfoundland. The pilot lived to tell the tale. Banting could not save his own life. What you stand for shapes how you live your life, how you treat others, how you run your business or career. It seeps into everything you do until it is seamless. People say, "Oh that's so *you*."

Here's a short list of things you might stand for, things that members of the Think Big Revolution stand for: women's rights, children's rights, education, animal welfare, literacy, justice, equality, humor, freedom, independence, respect, meaningful communication, less suffering, a sense of community, comfort, health, green living, self-expression, possibility, excellence, happiness, love, love, love.

Think about what you stand for . . . why do you do what you do ?

Don't intellectualize. When you overthink what you stand for, the energy leaks away. Your identity is driven by an inner passion, not a cold inner rationality. I'm not knocking rationality. It has its place, but it is not the core. Think *molten core* not *frozen core*. Once you have your *why-you-do-it* statement, you will know what you stand for.

There's a reason why you do what you do. Why you want to give the people in your *world* what you have to offer, to serve those around you. What you stand for is often general. That's okay. Once you can articulate the why of what you do, then you will achieve it all the better, because other people (most important, the people you want to serve) will get it. Or maybe they won't at first. That's why you have to live it. Because what you stand for is you, you will exhibit it in how you work and in how you live. That's what it really means to walk the talk. People will be excited about what you do only if you are excited about it. People will believe in you and what you do only if you believe. We need to set aside our trepidation and step out.

It can be scary to stand for something big and to let people know. Not to mention the fact that if you really stand for something, then it's not just words, it's work. Thinking big is always backed by good hard work. And that's scary, too.

I, Michael Port, stand for thinking bigger about who you are and what you offer the world. I want to think bigger in my own world and help others think bigger in theirs—after all, in the end we all live in the same world. Everything I do in my business and in my personal life is done with this ideology, this belief, at its core. I facilitate the Think Big Revolution. I wrote this book and others. I run a business that helps others achieve remarkable (and meaningful) business success. On the personal side, my lifestyle is designed so that I can help my son Jake think big about who he is and what he offers the world. I train in martial arts to achieve a higher excellence in my control over mind and body, which in turn increases my capacity for handling adversity.

Bruce Katz, the founder of Rockport, married work shoes and running shoes to create his megabrand of walking shoes. With his shoes, he helped give birth to the fitness-walking movement in the early 1980s. Bruce Katz stands for walking comfortably.

LensCrafters philanthropic initiative, The Gift of Sight, sums up what the company stands for: Clear vision is a basic human right, not a luxury.

John Wood, the founder and CEO of Room to Read, has built a global enterprise working with rural villages to build sustainable solutions to their educational challenges. Inspired on a trek through Nepal in 2000, he quit his comfortable senior executive position with Microsoft to pursue his dream of helping those without resources gain access to education. His vision is to provide educational access to 10 million children in the developing world. Room to Read has already begun working in Nepal, Vietnam, Cambodia, India, Sri Lanka, Laos, South Africa, and Zambia. Wood stands for educational opportunity for all.

When we know what we stand for, we can achieve big results in our world, whether it's building a giant brand, as Rockport and LensCrafters have done, creating a worldwide nonprofit, as John Wood did with Room to Read, or another less publicly visible goal.

Lisa Miller stands for helping women achieve their dreams. Her web address says it all: giveyourdreama-heartbeat.com. She knows about dreams. She worked hard to hang on to hers. Within a 10-month period in her life Lisa suffered the loss of her husband, her job, her home, and her dog, and she was in a car wreck that resulted in months of physical therapy. Lisa is an expert at healing and thriving in the face of adversity. As she says, "I've learned the ultimate level of success is the realization that you have everything you need right now, as you work toward goals and dreams. These two scenarios can coexist. If you're not happy now, you're not going to be happy when you have more money, purchase your dream home, or whatever goal you may have."

Paul Griffin stands for empowering teenagers to become leaders and forces of positive change in their families and in their communities. In the early 1990s, when his aspirations for a career in acting stalled out, he conceived the idea of a program that would bring teens from all walks of life (the inner city and the suburbs, white, black, Hispanic, and Asian, teens in stable homes and teens in foster care, the wealthy and the less privileged) together to create an original musical based on their lives. Now a nationwide teen-led and teen-driven nonprofit program in seven cities across the United States with more to come and in Israel and Cape Town, South Africa, City at Peace is developing an important presence and authority in the youth development and arts program community. Paul found (and followed) his true passion.

Shel Horowitz stands for keeping businesses honest. His first crack at fighting for what he believed in came in 2000, when he organized his community to preserve the local mountain against a completely inappropriate development plan that would have destroyed it. After reading an article in the local newspaper showing that the development plans were terrible and yet indicating that nothing could be done, Shel was galvanized. Within days, he had drawn up a petition, posted a web page, and called a community meeting. For months, he and a growing number of others fought the project on multiple fronts, from hydrology issues to the destruction of rare species to the slope of the proposed road, to name a few among a host of other problems. Soon the Department of Environmental Management opened an investigation into options for saving the land. "We had to persuade the public that a committed group of people can make a difference even when the experts said it was impossible," Shel says. He was right. The land was preserved. Now Shel Horowitz has moved on to broader initiatives. He has started a worldwide campaign to make crooked business dealings as unthinkable in a few years as slavery is today.

(Shockingly, as unthinkable as it is, slavery continues to exist in the United States and around the world. There are, according to some figures, as many as 17,000 slaves in the United States alone—sex workers, domestic workers, agricultural and manufacturing labor. Big thinking ended legal slavery. More big thinking is needed to end illegal slavery.) Shel's goal is to create a critical mass large enough to actually shift the consciousness of the business community. Although his campaign is not yet near his designated tipping point of 25,000 signatures, Shel says, "Already I'm seeing ripples in the culture." The green movement is one, and the growing emphasis on ethical business practices is another. "I like to think that I had at least a little to do with that beginning shift," Shel says.

Shel Horowitz isn't making boastful claims. He is thinking big and understands the power within each of us to make a difference when we really stand for something.

Kody Batemen stands for helping people become *card senders*—the kind of people who remember birthdays (on time, too), who send thank-you cards, *I'm thinking of you* cards, or *I appreciate our friendship* cards, not to mention the more prosaic variety of cards, such as *I hope you're still enjoying the boat I sold you* or *I enjoyed working with you*. Kody believes that people experience *promptings*, thoughts that pass through our consciousness one moment and are gone the next so that we don't act on them.

He knows.

Saying good-bye to his brother, after a regular family visit home to Utah in 1989, Kody didn't respond to a prompting to walk over and give him a proper hug. Three months later, his brother was killed, and Kody lived with the regret that he had not acted on his prompting. Kody founded SendOutCards.com to serve what he stands for, so others don't have to make the same mistake he did. Everyone in the company is always focused on this big picture—Kody's promise to help people act on their promptings and change the world into a more caring place. His employees share his vision, and he is helping them think bigger about who they are and what they have to offer the world.

Since its founding in 2003, SendOutCards.com/13009 (you can send a free a card on me) has grown to a company that does more than $10 million in business a year. Kody believes that we can never underestimate the power of our minds, the power of our ability to accomplish any goal.

Who do you know of, or know, who is a big thinker? Why do you admire that person? What does he or she stand for? What do you stand for?

You will (I guarantee you, and Kody probably would, too) succeed at a level you didn't think was possible when you know what you stand for and you live it. You will be bold and extraordinary, just being you. Your voice will be heard, because it is authentic, because you are honest with yourself and with others, and it will be evident. When we stand for something, we are who we are, no matter what.

As Henry Thoreau so beautifully wrote, "If one advances confidently in the direction of his dreams, and endeavors to live the life which he has imagined, he will meet with a success unexpected in common hours. . . . If you have built castles in the air, your work need not be lost; that is where they should be. Now put the foundations under them."

What are your castles? What do you value above all else? What is the last thing you would give up, and why? What do you dream of? What is your perfect world?

Statement of Core

I will identify what I stand for through a concerted process of self-questioning and exploration to discover my core, the *what* that is so *me*.

I will make public what I stand for.

I will hold myself visibly accountable each day to its letter and spirit.

1. OVERTHROW THE JUDGE (THE FRAUD FACTOR)

Control-alt-delete (it's not just for computers)—reboot yourself a judgeless world. Wash away the white noise, the ambient poison disseminated by the wild gremlins, the grim chorus of family, friends, colleagues, and others whose insidious chant of negativity has ensured the perpetuation of small thinking from generation to generation, from home to school, from graduation to retirement—*you can't do it, it's silly, it's been done before, you're not worthy, you're a fraud, you're wasting your time, why bother* . . . lies.

Recognize the lies. The so-called reality you are fed is nothing more than a media-mediated docudrama, a reenactment, an extreme makeover of the truth. Others do not always know better than you, quite the opposite.

To think big is to know there is no absolute knowing, except the knowledge that big things are possible.

Know that you cannot *know* (and neither can the so-called judges who have tried to pretend they have all the answers). You are not here to judge or be judged. If other people try to project their limited views of the world onto you, don't accept it. You are here to act with good purpose in the world, to tap into your own vital capacity to think big and do big things in the world.

Kimberly Rivers Roberts was born into poverty and disadvantage, to say the least. Her mother, a drug addict, died of AIDS, and by her early twenties Kimberly was selling drugs small-time and doing whatever else she could to get by. Her story was like that of too many others in the United States, land of opportunity that often offers no opportunity. She lived in a community dogged by persistent failure. Yet against all odds, Kimberly believed in herself. She wrote songs. One, titled *Amazing*, narrates the seemingly insurmountable obstacles she faced in her life, and yet the chorus keeps coming around again, "I'm amazing, I don't need you to tell me I'm amazing. . . ." That's overthrowing the judges. That's silencing the voices all around that conspire to keep us down. That's thinking big.

The day before Hurricane Katrina hit, Kimberly Rivers Roberts just happened to have bought a handheld video camera. She started filming her neighborhood—you guessed it, the Ninth Ward of New Orleans. Building on her chilling footage, documentary filmmakers followed her and her husband in the days and weeks that followed Katrina. The result is *Trouble the Water*, an electrifying film not just about the impact of Katrina, but about the power of hope in a country that has repeatedly disappointed those most in need. At the heart of the film are Kimberly's music and her refusal to give in to despair, her enormous capacity for generosity and forgiveness, and her love. Kimberly Rivers Roberts is a big thinker if ever there was one. We can all take a page out of her book. You're amazing. I'm amazing. We're amazing. We don't need anyone else to tell us we're amazing (though it's nice to hear, so always let people know when you think they're amazing, because thinking big means helping others to think big, too).

The number one judge you need to overthrow is the monster of your own mind, says my big thinking friend, Rick Carson, author of *Taming Your Gremlin: A Surprisingly Simple Method for Getting Out of Your Way*. As his title implies, it turns out that on the *judging* front, on the *you've-come-up-short* front, we are our own worst enemies. There is, as Rick puts it so nicely, a conversation that's always going on in our head between an angel and a gremlin. The gremlin gets his digs in, *"You've tried this before and it didn't work,"* while the angel tries to think big thoughts.

Rodney Cutler, a runner, triathlete, and owner of Cutler Salon in New York, calls this our personal CD. Sometimes the volume is turned way up and all we can hear is our negative thoughts: *You used to be faster. You're not just tired today, you're no good. You're too old now.* But when we're thinking big, the volume goes down on those small thoughts and big thoughts get tuned in and turned up.

I call this internal judge the Fraud Factor. It's a *disease* (or unease) with ourselves and who we are, and it's a *disease* (as in sickness). The good news: It can be treated. Our thoughts are like tiny warriors in our minds, engaged in a never-ending turf war, in the same way infection and antidotes are constantly duking it out inside our bodies. The Fraud Factor is the manifestation of the internal battle raging in our heads between small thoughts and big thoughts. Guess who's winning when we have a case of Fraud Factor, when we have a case of the *I'm-not-good-enoughs*?

Our worst enemy is staring out at us from the mirror every morning. What do we do about it? Well you've heard the saying, "Keep your friends close and your enemies closer." Observe the enemy. It is our own behavior. Does the enemy shrink from conflict? How does it feel when it does? Are the enemy's thoughts scattered or focused? Is it breathing fast or not at all? Play with these *natural* reactions. If the enemy breathes fast, we breathe even faster. If the enemy holds its breath, we'll hold ours longer. If we can accentuate our reactions to the gremlins and inject a sense of playfulness into our own behavior and responses to the judges, we will begin to strip away what's false. Get close to our inner selves. Deep down, underneath the CD track, past the chattering gremlin and the battlefield of tiny thought warriors, is you, the natural *you* (and me and us). What we stand for, our capacity to think big once all the noise is gone.

What is your noise? What is the conversation inside your head? From where do you get your negative messages? From you? From others?

Here's another angle. Instead of only trying to understand why we feel like a fraud from a psychological perspective (with all due respect to my parents and their worthy careers and my own wonderful therapist), look at the judges, the Fraud Factor, from an ontological point of view. Which means, instead of seeking to answer the question, "Why do I feel this way?" look directly at how you *are* with others. Ontology is about the nature of *being*. Ask yourself, "How do I behave in the world vis-à-vis this issue I feel a fraud about?" When we ask questions like this of ourselves, there exists the possibility that we can adjust our way of being without first obsessing on the deep issues underlying the behavior.

Here's a revolutionary thought: Sometimes it doesn't even matter why we are the way we are. Knowing may not help us change, anyway. How am I being in the world? That's a question that can help change our behavior. And, yes, sometimes, we also need to talk to a professional therapist about the psychological issues that affect our behavior. Beware of pandering when you do. Deal with reality.

How are you in the world? How do others see you? How do you see yourself? How are these two views different? How much of that difference is the judges?

You're wondering—how can we strip away what's false and find our core *and* take an ontological point of view as our guide? There's no contradiction. Understanding how our parents or peers may have screwed with our minds as a child is not the same thing as looking deep inside our hearts for what we stand for. The real you, the you of hopes and dreams, can be found whether or not you understand the complex psychology of why it was lost.

Above all, we need to value our own uniqueness, our own innate talents, gifts. On the one hand, we need to have enough self-esteem to believe we can do something and not give up. On the other hand, if we feel so great about ourselves that we see no need to strive to be better, then we stop creating, stop evolving, and that's no good, either. There's a balance to be struck between reality and possibility, between confidence and egotism. Finding the right mix is a matter of emotional intelligence. As we open ourselves up more and more to the world, we will also be developing our emotional intelligence to higher levels.

Shaking the Fraud Factor, having genuine confidence, comes with a feeling of being capable. Being capable is not the same thing as knowing lots of stuff. Having knowledge is not the same thing as capability. We are most often better off to face up to a challenge with the beginner's mind and the confidence of capability.

Lou Bortone has been in the television industry for more than 20 years; he is the founder of the Online Video Association. Early on in his career, one of his writing clients told him the secret was to "Fake it till you make it."

Says Lou, "I never agreed with that statement. I always believed that to be an *expert*, you truly had to be a master of your profession." By his own standard, he was never going to be an expert. Web technology was changing at breakneck speed, and he knew that he would never be able to claim to know it all. But then a funny thing happened. People began referring to him as the online video expert. Others decided for Lou that he was the expert. What did he learn? "As long as you're willing to keep learning, you can be an expert. Sometimes all it takes is staying a few steps ahead of the rest of the pack. You don't have to have all the answers, but you do need to keep asking the right questions."

Lou Bortone faced up to the challenge of being labeled an *expert* with a beginner's mind and confidence in his capability. No faking it. He had silenced his internal judge, the one telling him he would never be a master. Now he's thinking big.

Thinking small is often about who we think we *should* be. It's about a concept of a better self. But you are not a concept. I am not a concept. We are who we are and who we think we are. It's not easy to overthrow the judges and think big, but it's not complicated.

Once we've overthrown the internal judge, it's all that much easier to overthrow the external judges. Start with all the so-called gurus in your life. It's time to unhook, time to "de-guru-ize." (If you think that isn't a real word, it isn't. I made it up. Thinking big sometimes requires wild neologisms, and if that sounds a bit hoity-toity, *neologism* simply means "new word." Most of us make up words, aka neologisms, all the time. We just may not realize it. When you're thinking big, your new ideas might need new words.) End of deviation. Back to gurus, I'm not saying there aren't good, smart people with exciting, maybe even brilliant ideas worthy of an enormous amount of respect, perhaps even homage. What I am saying is this—no one is better than you.

Don't depend on other people for all your ideas. Explore and engage with other people's big thinking and inter-nalize it, make it right for you. Absorb what resonates. Pass on what does not. And add your own thoughts and ideas. Be independent and encourage independence in others. The more independent we are, the more loyal we can be to others. Dependence creates, well, *depend-ence*, not loyalty. To think big and to help others think big requires loyalty, a fundamental independence of thought and action.

When the judges have all been overthrown, you will realize your potential. Not the potential you always thought you had, but something bigger. As Marilyn Ferguson wrote some years ago in *The Aquarian Conspiracy*, "Our past is not our potential. . . . Whatever you may think about yourself and however long you may have thought it, you are not just you. You are a seed, a silent promise. You are the conspiracy."

What is your past? What is your potential? What is your silent promise?

Statement of Independence

I will be comfortable with who I am right now and know that I am good enough.

I will use my innate talents and gifts to do big things in the world.

I will not give up in the face of others' fear or disbelief.

1. COLLABORATE (TRUST EVERYONE. ALMOST)

Big thinking abhors a vacuum. Big thoughts necessarily feed at the same trough, draw on the same well, and thus, too, magically replenish the source by their taking.

Harry Potter's not the only one who gets a little magic in his life. What people can do together is beyond amazing, it is magical.

When your inward journey has progressed to a point of initial success (and I'm happy to report that the voyage never ends), when you know what you stand for and the judges are quieting, then you will begin to look outward with intent, in search of partners, of collaborators, of equals. You may, at first, seek out like minds. Eventually you will be a catalyst for others, helping them to think big, to escape the chains of their own small thoughts.

Riane Eisler writes this on the power of partnerships: that personal and political relationships based on domination inevitably result in misery and violence, whereas those founded on partnership foster respect, love, and an explosion of creativity. I couldn't agree more. Collaboration is the best of the future. Think of the digital world, where the old copyright model is giving way to new, open-source wiki models, musicians are bypassing the old record label model and releasing their songs online, authors are making available chapters of their books in progress, and there have even been collaborative writing projects in which authors have solicited feedback on early chapters to help them shape their focus and direction, none of which takes away from the individuality, creativity, or drive of these artists.

This book you are reading is a great example of the powers of collaboration. I wanted to write it in a very different style from my past books. I knew I needed help doing it, so I found Mina to work with me. My agent, Stephen Hanselman, and his partner, Julia Serebrinsky, were tough on the first few drafts of the book proposal, pushing Mina and I to do better. Once the book was in process, I solicited people from all over the place for their "think big" stories. When I needed input on ideas for the subtitle, I reached out to the members of the Think Big Revolution. Matt Holt, my publisher at John Wiley, was the one who best articulated what the book jacket ought to look like. And so many others offered important input all along the way. I couldn't be more grateful. If I had tried to do this alone it would never have been as good, if it had even happened at all.

In an interview, Randy Pausch says this of collaboration: "You can't get anywhere without help. That means people have to want to help you, and that begs the question: What kind of person do other people seem to want to help?" Pausch did not answer the question he posed, suggesting instead that the question itself was an answer to the existential question, *What kind of person do you want to be?* Nonetheless, I will answer the question more specifically: a big thinker, someone who believes in helping and being helped. That's the kind of person people want to collaborate with. *Being helped.* That turns out to be more difficult than *helping.* Too many people are unable to receive help. They are happy to help others, but when the coin is reversed it's a different story.

> True COLLABORATION is a give-and-take. True PARTNERSHIPS are founded in EQUALITY. Equality does not equal sameness. We don't all bring the same skills or RESOURCES to the table, but we all bring something and we all need something.

Thinking big means understanding that we alone are not in control, that we are not the only ones who can do it.

How often do you seek help? How open are you to receiving help?

Surround yourself with other big thinkers and experience the wonder of collaboration.

When you think big you will gravitate toward others thinking bigger. Helping yourself, you help others; they help you, and together you help the world. It's a circle, a roundelay, a boomerang, or any other shape or musical technique or game you can think of that comes back to itself in the end. It is one great, long jazz improvisation.

Jazz—that quintessential music of improvisational collaboration. How fitting, then, that so many big thinkers have risen in its ranks. Louis Armstrong (for one) was born at the rock bottom of the social ladder in a city of segregation, 1900s New Orleans. He grew up in circumstances that even the strongest of us would consider difficult. He got into trouble and spent time in a boys' home. But he transcended it all with the music he made in collaboration with so many others.

Jazz players feed off of each other. A theme on the piano becomes a riff on the guitar. The rhythm of the guitar becomes a drum solo. And they make music together that each would never have made singly. So it is with thinking big.

People who play big do so with others. When Brian Scudamore started 1-800-Got-Junk? he was a 19-year-old high school dropout sitting in a McDonald's trying to figure out how to maybe scrape together enough funds to go to college. He saw a beat-up old junk truck and thought,

"I could do that for some extra cash." Two years later he was collecting so much junk and making so much money that he dropped out college. From the beginning, he wanted to build something big, and he believed that together with collaborators in the form of franchise partners, they would be able to build something that much greater. 1-800-Got-Junk? is now a $100 million company. You may have seen some of their shiny, clean trucks around town, one of the hallmarks of Brian's marketing strategy. He knew that to play big, he needed other people.

People who play small think they have to do it all themselves. What about you? Are you ready to play bigger by truly collaborating with others? Or are you shut up in "silo thinking"? *Only I can do this right. I can't rely on anyone else. The way to get the job done is to do it myself.* The visual image of the grain silo, a tall, freestanding structure shut off from the rest of the farm operations, is often used as an analogy for businesses frustrated by departmental separations that have hardened into individual fiefdoms. No business can continue to meet the challenges of a changing world if its people don't communicate with each other. More, there must be genuine collaboration, not only in business, but in all aspects of life. Why would you want to separate yourself from others?

Big thinking breaks down the false separations that exist in the world—us and them, man and woman, adult and child, Asian, Caucasian, South Asian, African American, Hispanic, you-name-it, up and down, east and west. We are both us and them, one and the same interconnection, voluntarily or not. We are each inter-dependent individuals, part of a whole. When we are thinking small, we just don't know it, or we don't want to. Instead, we pursue the absurd notion that we are independent members of the same herd. What we really are is apart and adrift.

The paradox: Big thoughts create independence, not dependence. Big thinkers act instead of compete. They discover that in an open, fluid, back-and-forth collabora-tion, in the free flow of ideas, when you can entrust your-self to the notion of trust, big thoughts get even bigger.

"The very best rely on others," says Melani Ward, a business and marketing consultant to women. Melani helps powerful women "own their right to include oth-ers in their success." In a business world dominated by a hyper competitive mentality, too often the message is that "real success is what you create independent of others. Not only is that not true," says Melani, "it can be particularly toxic for women." Of course, men too, especially men who are thinking big, find the competition-mindset unhealthy and unproductive. Melani Ward helps others to see the deep value of collaboration. That's thinking big in the very best sense.

Collaboration releases us from the fear of doing things in the world, because we feel more comfortable with the obligation to deliver to a group who already supports what we're doing. That's why trust is essential. It is the foundation of any healthy partnership project.

Donald Trump Jr. likes to say that the number one rule his father taught him was "Don't trust anyone," including, apparently, his own father. Wow. That sounds like a fun way to go through life. I'm such a sissy, trusting my parents and all.

Trust is a big thing. That's why it takes big thinking. To learn to trust others requires first trusting yourself. The rest follows, although I won't say it necessarily follows naturally, because I know that for a lot of us instinctive distrust is deeply ingrained. I'm not saying you should trust everyone, always, without reservation. But as an opening gambit, everyone deserves our trust until they prove unworthy of it. Think of it as the *presumption of trust*, in honor of our great judicial rule, the presumption of innocence.

Partnerships are something we learn about as we go along—which is called *learning in action*. Keep trying different types of collaborations. If at first you don't succeed, well, it's not for life. It's not about long-term monogamy. If a partnership or collaboration works, great; if it doesn't, then it's time to move on. Moving on doesn't mean your collaborator was a bad person or, for that matter, that you were; it simply means that working together didn't meet each of your needs in the best way possible.

> In business terms, we each need to understand the VALUE PROPOSITION we bring to a project and what ASSETS we expect others to bring. It's not really so different from any other COLLABORATION: a friendship, a relationship, a training partner, a book group.

Collaborations are the hallmark of most supersuccessful companies. In fact, top companies tend to have been founded by slightly larger and more diverse groups. I don't mean the founders necessarily; it might be that the company has partnered with others on a project basis, thus profiting from project-by-project diversity.

We form partnerships and collaborations at three successive levels.

At the first level, we only engage in competitive interactions. We are on the offensive, or maybe the defensive. We are scared to share ideas, because maybe someone will criticize them, or worse, steal them. We have rigid boundaries and believe that there's one way of doing things—our way. We see things as win-lose. This competitive interaction is barely collaboration, if at all. If it works, it works despite itself. In the end it's just small thinking.

At the next level, we become capable of cooperative transactions, collaborations where we assign tasks among the group. You do this. I'll do that. I'll promote you if you promote me, and so on. There is more give-and-take than in a competitive interaction. These are transactions based in partnership, but are not a true partnership. The boundaries are selectively looser. But the bottom line is that we are protecting ourselves. Win-win is all right, as long as we win the same.

Big thinking strives for a higher level that consists of collaborative interactions. Rarely is this achieved in its pure form. Here, among big thinkers, is formed a partnership of open space, a free flow of ideas, in which boundaries are fluid. This kind of collaboration is possible only when we are very secure, win-win, without measuring who won more. Can we allow ourselves to be happy if we get what we want, even though others get more of what they want? It's not at our expense. There is no giant scorecard in the sky, and we shouldn't keep one in our heads. The very process of measurement suffocates openness and reinforces the negativity of competition. We are all winners if we can achieve a true collaborative interaction. Creativity on all sides is enhanced.

Collaboration levels: (1) COMPETITIVE interactions, (2) COOP-ERATIVE transactions, and (3) COLLABORATIVE interactions.

Joseph Jaworski, founder of Generon International, a leadership consulting company with clients worldwide, has devoted much of his life to the study and practice of leadership development. He founded the American Leadership Forum and is the author of the critically acclaimed book, *Synchronicity*. During his first year of college Joseph experienced a life-changing event that set the course of his passion and drive. Responding to a call for community help after a tornado hit town, Joseph worked for three days and three nights with a group of volunteers. "There was this sense of self-organization and distributed leadership. People seemed to know what to do without talking about it. There was a sort of collapse of boundaries," he says. The potential for re-creating this depth of teamwork and strength of leadership from within became his life's work. Joseph Jaworski believes that the realization of human possibility is achievable only through deep and true collaborations based on love and an open heart. Though he has a client list that includes some of the world's largest, most successful multinationals, some people think he's too radical, too *out-there*. Company leadership teams aren't meant to love each other. No? Why not? When we open our hearts, we open our minds. When we open our minds, then we can think big and then bigger. Love is at the foundation of the very best collaborations.

How do we find partners and collaborators? The same way you get a date. By believing in yourself and what you're doing. When you are excited about a project, you will draw others to you. You will receive offers of help. More than you can even accept. When you are aligned with your purpose, you can bring others in, because they see your excitement and feed off it. Your enthusiasm will nourish others and encourage them to join you in your effort. Your big thinking rubs off on others, and pretty soon you're helping others to think bigger about themselves and what they have to offer the world. Maybe you're already doing this on the Think Big Revolution web site. If not, do it now. Participate in and contribute to a revolution in progress, or start your own. Galvanize a group of people around an idea or an issue or a challenge that's not on our web site yet. We need you as our partner and collaborator at the highest level.

Are you the kind of person people want to help? Do you enjoy collaborating with others? What kind of collaborations do you engage in? Can you take your partnerships to the next level? Who do you love?

Statement of Collaboration

I will be a person others want to work with.

I will work with others without hidden or selfish intent to accomplish our mutual goals in the service of what each of us stands for.

2. GET COMFORTABLE WITH DISCOMFORT (IF THE SHOE PINCHES, IT FITS)

When we are thinking small, we crave preordained outcomes. We want to know what's going to happen before we begin. *Control is an illusion.* The need to know how and where prevents all progress.

Outcomes are not the starting point.

The twin demons of failure and rejection are mental illusions, the standard bearers of "excusitis." They sap our will. They suck away our energy. Pressures exist. Deal with it. To do big things in the world is dangerous and vital. Avoid control. Seek challenge. The more uncomfortable you are, the more challenged you are. Only then will you see the true liberation of breaking free from what you fear. It is life itself.

When we seek to control it, it's because we fear the unknown, the out of control. What we fear is reality, because ultimately it can never be controlled. The reality of reality is this: Every time we find an answer, so, too, we find a conflict with that answer. The closer we come to the core of a matter, of ourselves even, the more we realize the contradictions in the world and in our own nature.

Mina was married by the New York Society for Ethical Culture, an organization whose aim is to create a more humane society and one that believes that all individuals have the potential for growth and change and that with that potential comes a responsibility to help others realize their possibility. Big thinking. As Mina learned in the preparing-for-the-wedding process, it is also one that embraces the contradictions of the world. One of the exercises she and her partner were required to do before being married was to list the five things they loved most about each other. That was nice. Then they were asked to look at each of those five things and notice how what they loved most were the very things they disliked most about each other. Mina can be an infectiously energetic person, rallying others with her enthusiasm. She can also run over people with her energy, talking out of turn in her excitement, interrupting others before they're finished speaking. Two sides of the same coin. A contradiction. Unavoidable.

An aside: I attended the Ethical Culture Fieldston School in New York, which was founded on the same philosophical principles that govern the Society for Ethical Culture, and I was nurtured throughout childhood to accept the inevitability of contradiction. Not, of course, that I don't still struggle with it—a lot.

What are your greatest strengths? What are your greatest weaknesses? How are the two related?

Until we can understand our own contradictions, we cannot understand those of others. Until we understand the contradictions in others, we cannot understand the contradictions of the universe. We will seek to control, in vain. We will look for comfort and find discomfort. Better, then, to get comfortable with discomfort. Spend your valuable energetic resources on thinking big instead of fighting reality.

Another contradiction about fighting reality, from my life: I have trained in the art of aikido since 1996. I have a black belt, but belts are just used to hold up your pants. The style of aikido I practice is one of the very traditional martial arts, a discipline for training the mind and body. While it is a martial art, the way we train is not always realistic. Meaning, in a modern-day street fight, aikido is generally not considered your best defense. I recently added Brazilian (Gracie) Jui-Jitsu training to my regimen, to learn the skills of ground grappling, which are more appropriate for the reality of fighting. Do I plan on fighting? Of course not. In fact, Buddhist thought influences my training in aikido and beyond. And, as a Buddhist friend of mine recently said, how many Buddhists get into street fights? While I'm not a Buddhist, I certainly respect and believe in the ultimately peaceful goals of Buddhism and value the mental and physical strengths that are the goals of aikido. Yet I want to feel complete in my training, to fully embrace reality, and because it is a good feeling, to know I can protect myself (and others) if need be. It's also just plain fun to be tested on a daily basis. That's what big thinkers do; they are willing submit to testing, again and again.

I hope never to have to use my training in an actual fight. I want the skills to feel strong and capable inside myself, not to impose my strength on others. We may have the most loving nature, but there will be times when we are called on to fight for what is right. We need to know how to fight—and that will mean different things to different people. Gandhi fought with civil disobedience. I derive mental strength from knowing that I am strong physically. It is with this mental fortitude that I face the challenges life offers. Being strong is essential to facing the contradictions of reality and thinking big.

This is the warrior mentality. No, that's not a male thing. Being a warrior is not about being a tough guy, being a fighter, or endorsing violence. I mean it in the yogic sense, that combination of strong and gentle that is the hallmark of yoga practice. When we are warriors, we understand that there is no control, that the world is a chaotic place, but that this "control-less-ness" is not necessarily confusion. In fact, clarity in the midst of this chaos comes when we learn to let go—to let go of our need to control and instead open ourselves to the world and its endless potential.

To think big is to love the universe, to embrace our passion. To love is to fight for what we love. What a waste not to, when we have only this one life to live.

Death is a destination we all share, like it or not. "Time is all you have . . . and you may find one day that you have less than you think," as Randy Pausch wrote. Would you rather think small, succumb to a wasteful subexistence, living others' lives? Would you rather play it safe? You might just as well bury yourself early—or how about now? So what if someone makes fun of you? So what if someone tells you that you're crazy to even try? So what if in fact you do fail?

When best friends Heather White and Lori Joyce started a cupcake bakery in Vancouver, Canada, with no baking or restaurant experience, they leased out space in a high-rent, high-turnover, seasonal district. The risk was big. So, too, was their thinking. Their first summer it seemed like more people came through the front door just to tell them that they would be closed in a few months. It was discouraging. Yet it also gave them the strength to prove the naysayers wrong. As friends, they believed in each other. Heather and Lori didn't succumb to the small thinking negativity of others. They are driven, passionate, and devoted, and they believed (and continue to believe) they can do anything. Cupcakes by Heather & Lori sells retail and wholesale cupcakes, cakes, and other goodies. The company now has three locations and more than 50 staff, and that's certainly not the last you'll hear of Heather and Lori. They're still thinking big. Once you've started, you won't stop. Ever.

Often, we believe that thinking bigger brings bigger problems. You want to start your own business, but you can't let go of your stable job, paycheck, house, car, and so on. Those considerations appear to be big roadblocks to your success. Not so. That's just fear of what others will think. When Brandon Hartsell and his business partner, Nicole Shaw, started Sunstone Yoga, they sank every penny into the enterprise and lived in the studio. If those sound like big risks and big problems, having little money and no home, then redefine success. Brandon and Nicole were driven by passion. They dared to dream. They thought big. Sunstone Yoga, now a string of popular studios in Dallas, Texas, is consistently named as "Best in Dallas."

We cannot let the fear of discomfort stop us (to paraphrase something John McCain said long before he was a presidential hopeful). The pain of remorse, of wasted opportunity, is a cancer far worse than any of the pain or humiliation we so fear when we are thinking small.

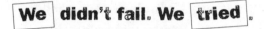

We didn't fail. We **tried**.

Challenge and capacity feed on each other in a symbiosis, a cycle of exponential growth; as we begin to think big, our big thoughts blossom. So go ahead, increase discomfort. Increase candor.

As we become more comfortable with discomfort, so our capacity to do big things increases. Know that if what makes us uncomfortable seems small, it's not the same thing as small thinking. Each challenge is our worthy opponent. As we take on bigger challenges, so the next larger challenge becomes more manageable. The more we overcome, the more we can overcome.

There are no three easy steps, but when we become comfortable with discomfort, we will accomplish great things. We will feel *high* on the abundance of life.

For some, the discomfort is not in the starting, but in the success and in the expectations that come with achievement. It's just another way of being uncomfortable. We can never stop striving to think big. In writing this book, I've taken myself to task. I set my own personal bar that much higher. If I am to remain a credible author of *The Think Big Manifesto*, I cannot flinch in the face of discomfort (as much as I may want to and still do sometimes). With this manifesto, I'm challenging you and me to become comfortable with discomfort, to think bigger.

Three things we will do:

(1.) Improve and act on our intuition, which is our highest intelligence and derives from our place of truth. This is to *up* the visibility of our purpose, what we stand for. Such candor in turn will make us more accountable and increase the number of situations that make us uncomfortable.

Ouch.

(2.) Improve our promises. When we think big, we promise to deliver a remarkable outcome. The pressure is on.

Uncomfortable pressure.

(3.) Take more risks, a lot more. It takes daring to invest in ourselves and others, but it will bring us to that place of great discomfort faster, that place where we can accomplish big things. It's too easy to live with the daily, small, inertial discomforts of avoiding our fears. Risk induces activity. Activity disperses fear and inertia. As a Japanese proverb says, "Fall down seven times, stand up eight."

Candor, promises, risks; at first it's like a giant shot of wasabi—all that accountability, all that visibility. It's going to sear our nostrils with every breath and make our scalps sweat—all the better (and if you have a head cold, presto, it will be gone, too). Once we're thinking big, we will call like-minded people to action: Rock the boat. Maybe it sinks. Maybe it needed to sink.

Think: Will I rise up and put myself in consistently uncomfortable situations in order to think big about what I offer the world, even if every fiber of my being tells me to sit down and shut up?

Yes.

Comfort is a relic.

What's inside your comfort zone? What's outside? What makes you uncomfortable? Why?

Statement of Discomfort

I will not seek control.

I will make visible my purpose, make promises in its service, and take risks to fulfill my commitments.

3. PROMISE AND FULFILL (SAY YOU WILL ... AND DO)

Promises. Promises. Does the very word make you uncomfortable? Conjure up images of promises forgotten, broken, or never fulfilled? If promises don't make us uncomfortable, then we haven't been trying hard enough. Or we haven't been taking our promises seriously. A promise without delivery is worse than no promise at all.

Promises are, to some extent, uncomfortable because you have to keep them. Sure, sometimes they can be and may need to be renegotiated. But, ultimately, when you promise and commit, someone is counting on you. Someone is, maybe many someones are, expecting you to deliver something. When we say we'll do something, then we will. We won't just *try* to make good on our word, we will fulfill what we have undertaken. Possibly more. Too many avoid making promises in the first place, fearing the accountability, preferring to hide under a cloak of diminished expectations. How often have we heard (or said) the words, *I can't promise you that I'll do it, but I'll try*. Why would we want to live in the half-light, of such a soft engagement with others and the world?

We will make promises **. Big promises. Promises hard to fulfill. Yet we will—** fulfill **.**

Teddy Roosevelt said it well in a 1920 speech he delivered at the Sorbonne in Paris, "It is not the critic who counts, not the man who points out how the strong man stumbled, or where the doer of deeds could have done them better. The credit belongs to the man who is actually in the arena; whose face is marred by dust and sweat and blood; who strives valiantly; who errs and comes short again and again; who knows great enthusiasms, the great devotions, and spends himself in a worthy cause; who, at the best, knows in the end the triumph of high achievement; and who, at worst, if he fails, at least fails while daring greatly, so that his place shall never be with those cold and timid souls who know neither victory nor defeat."

To promise and fulfill is to be the doer of deeds, not the critic. It is to be fully in the world, not standing apart or hovering above. We are in the ring, on the stage, open to being judged, but not judging.

When John Allen Mollenhauer started his company, Performance Lifestyle Solutions, several years ago, he was, as he says, "thinking big all right, but it was more like a big bang when my starry-eyed thoughts shot out in every direction. . . . I had a universe of projects and wasn't able to follow through fully on most of them." He had a world of opportunity, but he was driving himself into the ground and he was not fulfilling his commitments. Now he's learned that underlying the need to promise and fulfill is the fundamental principle of managing personal energy. As he says, "I've learned that focused action requires powerful personal energy and that it needs to be managed well. Feeling powerful enables me to make commitments and follow through."

When we know we must fulfill the promises we make, by necessity we are forced to harness our own energy to that end, to ensure we are capable of doing what we say we'll do. That's not the same thing as making easy promises or promising things that are easy for us to fulfill.

To promise in comfort is not to promise.

Bring on the discomfort by making your promises public, for others to hear and see; only then will you get out of no-man's land, out of that in-between place of moderate comfort and low motivation.

What's the most recent promise you made? What's the most recent promise you broke?

About 10 years ago, Beryl Katz, then a stay-at-home mother who was feeling out of practice at being in the so-called real world, had an idea. It was this—to unite youth and seniors in a quest to enrich education. She thought through her idea and finally went with a friend to the superintendent of schools to share her idea. Her plan was to inspire the school district to take on the challenge and make her idea happen. The superintendent loved the idea. He asked who would make the idea a reality, and Katz's friend pointed at her. As Beryl says, "Yikes . . . I never thought I would be able to take an idea from its infancy and see it through to becoming a self-sufficient adult!" But she did. In 1999, Senior Adults for Greater Education (S.A.G.E.) was born. The organization now places more than 150 weekly volunteers in classrooms across Bucks County, Pennsylvania. Even more volunteers give their time on an episodic basis, helping students with reading, mathematics, and science; guest lecturing on subjects ranging from personal experiences with eating disorders to archaeology; and teaching students to play chess and knit. "I am accountable to the volunteers," Beryl says. "I am accountable to our students, seniors, and school."

It wasn't what she expected and, at first, it wasn't comfortable. But Beryl Katz fulfilled the promise she offered when she came up with her idea for S.A.G.E.

Susan Spitzer, a lawyer who coaches other lawyers on how to open their own practices says, "There was a time in my life when I didn't keep many of my commitments. I was so embarrassed that I stopped making them altogether." Well, that's not going to work, and Susan knew she was missing out on life. So she made a deal with herself. "You can break any commitment you make as long as you disclose the absolute, honest truth for backing out to the person or people affected." The result? Susan is careful about the commitments she makes (as all big thinkers should be), and she rarely breaks commitments. None of us are perfect. Here's an example of what Susan did recently when she had to break a commitment.

"I was asked to advise a group of middle school kids participating in a mock trial. I met with their teacher and learned about the program and her expectations of me. I was in over my head. I am not a trial attorney. I had to get out for both myself and the kids. I told the teacher and the person who recruited me that this was beyond my skill level. However, I made telling the truth easier by lining up an assistant district attorney to take my place."

Fulfilling real promises will involve discomfort. But it should be the discomfort of a genuine challenge, not the discomfort of being truly unequipped. Susan Spitzer recognized this and had the wisdom to know when to break a commitment that had gone awry. Fortunately, she still fulfilled the promise to the school kids. They got a capable attorney to participate in their mock trial, just not the one originally expected.

Making commitments and fulfilling them also means getting over the need to be perfect or right all the time. As Tina Forsyth, cofounder of OnlineBusinessManager .com says, "If I try to do everything right I'll never get anything done. Instead, just get out there and do it . . . and if it needs to be fixed or upgraded, that can always be done later." That's not to say we should fulfill our promises sloppily. Certainly not. We do the absolute best we can and know that if we can do even better later, we will revisit and top up the fulfillment of our original promise. Sometimes, just knowing that we don't have to be perfect gives us the room to breathe when we need to fulfill a particular commitment. Tina, for example, recommends the following, "I play a little trick on myself to get creative projects done, such as writing projects. If I sit and try to write the finished product, I usually get stuck and spin my wheels trying to make it work. If I tell myself, 'I'll just write a draft first,' the words start to flow." It turns out that when we take some of the pressure off, we can get a lot more done. We need to promise in discomfort, but not so much so that we stop doing anything.

Big thinkers invite challenge. We welcome discomfort. It can be our motivation, our catalyst. We look discomfort directly in the eye and let the light of the promises we make burn like the noon sun. And when our retinas are good and fried, we will have replenished our capacity and authenticity and, with that, our ability to do big things.

Do you make promises you know you can fulfill with ease? Do you make hard promises? Do you make promises you know you can't fulfill (even if you wanted to)?

Statement of Promises

I will be an authentic person, one whom others can rely on.

I will make hard promises that push me to the best of my capacity.

I will not just try to fulfill. I will.

5. SUBMIT TO AUTHORITY TO BE AN AUTHORITY (LISTEN MORE, TALK LESS)

The future belongs to the learner, not the learned, not the teachers who have lost their own will to learn. To know is not to know anymore. To think big is to lead by learning, to lead by example.

> If you STAND FOR something, then it will GUIDE everything you do, and so you will naturally set an EXAMPLE.

People who think small try to lead by teaching others to do things their way, thus perpetuating an inertial downward spiral of hierarchical pedagogical dogma—in other words, *I'm-better-than-you-listen-to-me-this-is-the-only-right-answer*. Small thinking people can rarely hear the sound of anything but their own voices.

Nothing is heard until the ego is transcended (not an easy task). To listen is to lead.

It sounds contradictory: You need to follow rules to be followed. You need to submit to be submitted to. It only seems so. In fact, there is no contradiction; rather, there is a unity, an integrity that comes from this principle. By imposing parameters on ourselves, we set ourselves free. Outer discipline coincides with and is synonymous with inner discipline. There is no private you and public you. You need to *be* in public what you *are* in private—that is what it means to live authentically. You want to be authentic, don't you? I'm pretty sure there aren't too many people who *want* to be fake, and those who are, or who seem to be, are more likely just scared of putting themselves out there, of letting the public see the genuine person who lives inside them. We fear that our ego (our true self, with all our dreams and hopes, our very identity) will be crushed if we take a risk, if we put ourselves out there. Then we are not living authentically. Fear of censure may keep some from authenticity, but in our hearts, if we let our hearts speak, we all yearn to be authentic.

You are authentic when you submit to self-imposed rules, codes of conduct based on what you stand for.

To be free , is to be bound by something bigger than yourself.

From the scarcity naturally created by restrictions comes abundance. You can husband your internal reserves for doing big things.

When we think small about authority, we contradict ourselves. *Do as I say, not as I do.* When you think small your energy is dissipated fighting against authority for the sake of the fight. In the process you end up unwittingly subjugating yourself to a wasteful cycle of confrontation and competition. If we spend all our time fighting the rules, how much time and energy will we have left to get up to big things? Don't deplete yourself. Thinking big is hard work, and you'll need all your energy. Relax. Submit a little.

What rules did you break this week? This month? This year? What rules did you make for yourself? What rules do you follow?

What does it really mean to submit? Does it mean to follow a direction set down by someone else? Sometimes. Of course, blindly following an unjust authority is not the kind of submission I'm recommending. History has proven time and again that to be a follower when every fiber of your body cries out against the capriciousness of the authority is likely the wrong path to take.

But authority in and of itself is not unjust. Excluding the capricious (or worse) authority just mentioned, not all rules are inherently bad. How often do we buck rules for the sole purpose of feeling special or to get something more easily than someone else? Every time we break a rule for our own personal gain, when we take shortcuts, we directly and proportionately reduce the respect others will have for us. In honoring others' authority, we set an example of how we, too, ought to be respected.

A quick clarification of meaning: By *shortcuts*, I mean quick fixes, half measures, patch jobs, and Band-Aid solutions. That's a very different thing than finding a more efficient way to do something. That's not a shortcut. It's a whole new process or way of being. That's not breaking a rule. That's discovering a new and better rule, which in turn we submit to as we go forward.

Alexis Martin Neely is a lawyer who discovered a better way of practicing her career and has made it her mission to show others how to do so, too. But she couldn't do it until she'd submitted to the authority of the big law firm she started out with when she graduated from law school. As a young associate lawyer, Alexis found that law firm life was all about image and doing what she was told. Her life was not her own. It was painful, and she frequently felt as though she was missing a major part of herself. But, as she says, "I had to experience all of that to become the authority on helping lawyers break free of the broken business model that had most of them trapped in perpetually unfulfilled lives." Fortunately for Alexis, she could see the road ahead early on. She knew that nothing would change unless she did. So she did. Now she helps others to do what she did. Alexis Martin Neely's passion for changing industry standards and her innovative approach to client service and estate planning has earned her many accolades, including Super Lawyer Rising Star in *Los Angeles* magazine and one of *Worth* magazine's Top 100 Lawyers. Neely understands that sometimes submitting is the right thing and sometimes changing the rules is the way forward.

We might look at submission in this way—to follow a direction set down by a thoughtful authority whose authenticity and integrity we respect. From this perspective, it takes on a different hue. When we submit, we should not be subjugated. The real question we should ask ourselves is this: Am I here to learn? There is almost always something to be learned by submitting to authentic authority that is exercised with integrity. If you'd rather just do things your way . . . well, maybe you're reading the wrong book. The most dangerous words I know are: *I know that.*

There are times when, for our own good or the good of society, we need and ought to submit to a force larger than self. It could be a coach or a teacher. It could be submitting to the dynamic of a group to which you belong, a business partner, your AA sponsor, or the Weight Watchers program you just joined. More dramatically, it could be submitting to the wisdom of someone who seems to be in a *lesser* position than you. When the *Challenger* disaster happened in 1986, seven people died, including a schoolteacher. Horribly, in the course of the investigation into why the rocket disintegrated shortly after liftoff (and in front of the eyes of millions of television viewers), it was discovered that line engineers had wanted to postpone the space mission, as they believed there was a 1 in 100 chance that certain O-rings (a sort of rubber washer) were not reliable in colder temperatures. Warnings were ignored by top managers of the mission, who were too busy *thinking big* about their space mission to be concerned by what those down the line were saying.

Authority does not always come from the top down, not even most of the time. And thinking big is not about barreling ahead to win (it isn't even about winning), throwing caution to the wind. Thinking big includes considering the risks, to yourself and others. Yes, we need to get comfortable with discomfort and take risks. No, we should not and cannot (as big thinkers) take foolish risks simply for the sake of glory, particularly if the lives of others are at stake (which they will be, because if we are thinking big, chances are we are doing so in conjunction with others).

Still, to subscribe to a plan, to a *way* of doing things, often feels uncomfortable. The top brass in the *Challenger* mission apparently thought that the public relations repercussions of postponing the mission would be too uncomfortable to bear. But one of the more common reasons we don't like submitting is because often we confuse rebellion and revolution. To rebel instinctively against all authority is not revolutionary. Unless your goal, like James Dean's, is "to live fast, die young, and leave a beautiful corpse," being a rebel without a cause is jumping a fast train to nowhere. Yet when we are revolutionary, which we all are when we start thinking big, we need to be open to the world of new ideas. Open and disciplined. Confident and willing to learn. Authoritative and submissive. Inherent contradictions creating a unity of purpose and action.

We can never truly collaborate with others if we are not willing at times to submit to the will of the group. To truly, fully learn, we must be open and willing to hear others, to submit to their expertise.

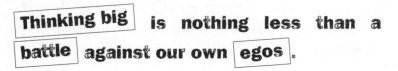

Thinking big is nothing less than a **battle** against our own **egos**.

Our egos may even fight against our own self-imposed rules. When Michael Dalton started his business, Guided Innovation Group, he was advising clients on how to find and profitably serve the unmet needs in their niche. Meanwhile, his own marketing was geared to appeal to almost any company and his communications were written to keep the door open no matter who walked through it. Michael says, "I realized

I wasn't submitting to authority . . . I wasn't taking my own medicine. It was time to submit and let go of the security blanket of an overly wide market definition." Now Michael clearly focuses on his target market: CEOs and business unit managers of midsize or larger manufacturing and technology-based companies in which there is either a shortage of resources or a level of dissatisfaction with the organic growth rate and/or percentage of sales made up of new offerings. "With a clear picture of my audience, everything just seemed to get easier—my networking, my marketing, my writing," Michael says.

When we submit, we transcend our ego. If we can't get beyond our own egos, then it will hold us back from doing big things. But, but, but . . . the ego is also the thing that allows us to do big things. As with everything, there is a point of balance, a zone between flexibility and self-discipline that will be different for each of us. The challenge is to submit and yet still be discerning. To submit, yet maintain our individuality, to not get drawn into the dangerous waters of groupthink and herd mentality. How you find this balance is guided by your own authenticity and integrity.

I navigate this balance almost daily in my practice of aikido. I must submit to my martial arts teacher and at the same time build up my own sense of self vis-à-vis my practice. Achieving in martial arts is often a matter of breaking yourself down to cut through the layers of fat persona hiding the core of true strength beneath.

In the end, our self-discipline must manifest itself in this way: We do what we say we're going to do. Our actions are in accord with our intentions. Public and private are married in one inward/outward unity. Integrity is being congruent. Our thoughts are not in conflict with our actions. The plumber's pipes may leak and the shoemaker's wing tips may have holes in the soles. These homey adages do not describe the person living in integrity. Blame my martial arts training, but I like to call this big thinking person the master.

> The true MASTER is someone who does in private what they do in public. The master is a LEADER and a FOLLOWER, always a LEARNER.

The relationship between parent and child is one in which finding this balance is crucial. As a parent, you must do as you teach. While I lay no claim to great parenting expertise, I believe that children (like adults) need some rules and authority. Not rules and authority of the "do this because I said so" variety. Children cannot grow into their own individuality without some explanations. Their questions need to be answered. Even more important, the behavior that parents desire of their children must first and foremost be modeled by the parents. At the same time, neither children nor adults can spend their whole life questioning. If we do that, then we are always judging. There are times and places where it is appropriate to submit without excessive questioning. Children can understand this, and the children who trust their parents will know there are times to submit without question or controversy.

So choose your teachers wisely. It is a great good to be surrounded by people (parents, teachers, colleagues, and friends) who create constraints in our lives in the service of higher goals.

In integrity we have authority. Through submission we have authority. With authority we help others do big things in the world.

What have you taught others lately? What have you learned from others?

Statement of Submission

I am here to learn.

I will deliberately seek out wise and true teachers and submit to the authority of the constraints they create in the service of our goals.

8. LIVE IN INTEGRITY (DOES IT NEED TO BE SAID?)

Be congruent in purpose and action. Find the convergence and coalescence of full self-expression. Maybe you've lived until now in a maelstrom of conflict and self-inhibition, trying to control things that at best can only be influenced. That's thinking small. Maybe you've thought that being consistent is enough, without considering the content of your consistency. Just because you have goals and stick to them doesn't mean you are thinking big. If your goal is to stay out of trouble, to keep your head down, to raise no eyebrows, to get through the weeks until the next paycheck, you're thinking small. You are not doing justice to yourself or others.

Not only should we all think bigger about who we are, too many other people stand to benefit from what you can offer the world for you not to think bigger.

Maybe you are wildly successful in your career and you've made a billion dollars, but you haven't spent a weekend with your children for months, and you're letting the treadmill of making ever more money and climbing ever higher on the corporate ladder rule you when you should be ruling yourself. You're thinking small about what you can get out of life.

> Thinking big is HOLISTIC. It is internal and external congruency. It applies at home and at work, and inside your THOUGHTS and out in the world. That is INTEGRITY and it is how we will live when we think big.

For years Debra Costanzo worked in a series of wrong jobs. She was employed in positions that offered money but no personal fulfillment. Ironically, in many of her jobs that were related to human resources and placement, Debra was advising young people to train themselves for a career they would be willing to do for free. "I was dead serious," she says. "The only problem was that I wasn't following my own advice. I always took the safe route." Debra was living without integrity in her work. She was miserable. What she really wanted was not manifested in what she was actually doing. Then she discovered this big thinking truth, "If you stop telling yourself 'when I *start* doing . . . ' and change the thinking to 'I *am* doing . . . ' things will really start to happen for you! So often we think of ourselves as *planning* to develop rather than thinking of ourselves as *developing*. . . . We don't feel worthy of the 'I am doing' moment. Rather, we explain ourselves away by staying in the 'when I start doing' moments. It's safer. . . . It's self-sabotage." Debra Costanzo is doing now, instead of waiting to start doing.

To live without integrity is to purposefully diminish your own chance of success, your chance of contributing in the biggest way you can to the world.

In the end, our integrity is all we have. It is our value. In business, it is the foundational building block of our marketing. To be without integrity is fundamentally damaging to our ability to think big and do big things in the world. We need to stay vigilant against the least downward slide. *I'll just do this one thing, then I'll get back to . . .* Don't become a politician. Our lives should not be a series of compromises with the various factions lobbying for our attention or energy. There are side effects: our future, for one thing, and the future of others, for another.

George Orwell once said, "In a time of universal deceit, telling the truth is a revolutionary act." What truths will you tell? How will your integrity be made manifest?

Casey Truffo is a licensed marriage and family therapist in California. She left a well-paying position as a corporate vice president to become a psychotherapist because she wanted to help people. It turns out that one of the groups she's helping now is other therapists. When she started out she discovered through personal experience that no one was helping therapists when they started out. She believed that no one was providing the kind of advice they needed to start their practices, nor was it considered in good taste to focus on those issues. Building a practice to a certain level of success was frowned upon. A therapist was not supposed to do well financially. A virtuous therapist was supposed to be poor. To be a therapist required one to be self-sacrificing, including financially. Casey believed that therapists had as much right as any other health care professionals to be wealthy.

At the time she started saying it, Casey was considered a heretic—that is, someone who expresses ideas contrary to accepted, orthodox doctrine. She was really a *revolutionary*. She applied to speak at conferences and was turned down. "I was accused of horrible things like trying to gouge clients. I even toyed with changing the name of my company (BeAWealthyTherapist.com) to something more benign to avoid the controversy." She didn't. Casey stayed true to herself and her integrity. "The controversy led me to a bigger calling, to change the notion that therapists needed to be poor." Casey Truffo is "happy to report that this 'poverty identity' among therapists is beginning to change," and she is "delighted to be a part of something so big." Her goals are evolving, "Now my mission is to help therapists, and the profession of therapy, get respect from the general population."

Live in integrity, true to yourself. It matters, to you, to me, and to everyone. We live in a networked world, a world of connections. What we do has an effect on others and what others do has an effect on us. For more than a century we've understood that contagious disease can spread through our networks, but now it turns out that networks propagate and amplify behavior, too, both negative and positive, and not only disease-inducing behavior. We don't just spread colds to those around us, we can spread obesity, or the will to quit smoking, or the desire to change the world. Habits, good and bad, spread through networks like a virus. We are inclined to adopt the habits of those closest to us.

Our values and actions are contagious.

When we think big, it is contagious. But beware: When we or others think small, the influence is that much more virulent. As much as we influence others, so are we at risk of *catching* others' values and actions, of coming under their influence. If we surround ourselves with small thinkers, we will think small.

Remember this, too: We are our own most dangerous source of contagion. It is our own small thoughts that can act most virulently against our big thoughts. As Frances Hodgson Burnett wrote 100 years ago in her still beloved children's book, *The Secret Garden*, " . . . [T]houghts—just mere thoughts—are as powerful as electric batteries—as good for one as sunlight is, or as bad for one as poison. To let a sad thought or a bad one get into your mind is as dangerous as letting a scarlet fever germ get into your body. If you let it stay there after it has got in you may never get over it as long as you live."

The irony is this: The negative energy and influence of small thinking ripples outward through our networks with a force greater than the positive energy of big thinking. Small thinking has the power to suck in everything around it. To influence and sway small thoughts, big thinking must at first exert twice the strength to achieve a fraction of the same force. Bad news.

Good news: Everything has side effects. The negative energy of small thinking is preset to autodestruct in its own entropic circle of influence. Negativity can prevail only so long. In the end it feeds on itself so ferociously that it will consume itself. At the basest level, a network spreading disease (whether a cold or obesity or cancer) cannot long survive its own natural demise. So, too, a network spreading *dis*-ease and small thinking will ultimately close in on itself under the weight of its negativity.

We are all part of different networks. Our influence is more than we think. It matters that we think big, because others around us are affected by our thinking and being and actions. And we are influenced by the others' thoughts more than we know. It matters to think big, to protect against the negative influences we may encounter. We must don our mental crampons against the slippery slopes of negativity and compromise. Gird ourselves against the great negativistic vacuum that will eventually create a black hole where once there were small thoughts. Only by thinking big, fiercely, ferociously, with all our will, can we withstand this vacuum.

> When we think big we are aware at all times of what we are INFLUENCING and what influences us. We undertake to bring POSITIVITY to RELATIONSHIPS, but we will not take away others' negativity. We give what we give, but we are careful about what we take away. Relationships are not transactional.

We are connected to others, but we are not, and should not be, attached. We are under no obligation to take on someone else's issues or absorb others' negativity. As we begin to think bigger, our networks may change. Yes, our friends, lovers, and colleagues may change. We will need to make serious decisions about those we can keep in our lives and those we cannot. Just as we draw people to us with our values and actions, so we will shed those who are not yet ready to think big, who cling to small thinking.

Who brings you down? Who makes you feel good? Who in your life thinks small? Who in your life thinks big?

Amanda is a regular on the Think Big Revolution weekly call. When she started thinking big, opening her own business, her husband of 20 years didn't support her efforts. He was jealous of her dream (not to mention her budding success) and obstructive of everything she tried to do. She realized that his behavior was simply a continuation of his generally abusive behavior toward her over the course of their marriage. Not only did Amanda think big enough to build her own business, she tackled the next challenge and left her unhealthy marriage.

There is a myth about success: that those who achieve it leave many behind. Perhaps a few who achieve success are like this; more often, though, it is envy or ill will that prevents the less successful from following their friends. We may fear success because we are not comfortable with how those around us will deal with our success. That's thinking small, on both sides. When we think big, we will succeed, and we cannot fear the advent of success and its side effects. We must be ready to leave behind those who will not support us, who will not celebrate with us, just as we would celebrate their successes. We are never held back from big thinking by others. We hold ourselves back by allowing others' influence to negatively affect us.

We will refuse to adopt the negative values and habits of those around us: our lover who is depressed and causes us to be depressed; our friend who gossips about, envies, and criticizes others and encourages us to do the same; and our colleague who cuts corners, procrastinates, and does the minimum amount necessary to maintain the status quo.

We will break with negative influences. But it must be done consciously and specifically to be effective. *I can't be around you right now. It's just not the right energy for me.* Harsh? Possibly. Healthy? Yes. We cannot think big if we are surrounded by small thinking, negative influences, and bad habits: the friend who *supports* us, but doesn't believe in us; the partner whose lifestyle is unhealthy; the business colleague who takes comfort in mediocrity.

We will be a positive influence and we will surround ourselves with positive influences. That's what big thinking is and what it requires. Ron Quintero grew up in the foster care system and spent some time living on the streets. He might have settled into his comfortable UPS job, which offered secure benefits and a decent wage, but he didn't. He quit UPS to pursue his dream of a career in real estate. He ran through his savings, and his home went into foreclosure. His girlfriend stuck with him. She supported him and believed in him. She thought big with him. Now Ron Quintero is the founder of My Resource Center, Mortgage Leaders Edge, Debt Advisory Alliance, and Finance This Home, a suite of highly successful businesses.

We cannot change others, only ourselves. We can hope to influence them only by the integrity of our own behavior and actions. There's so little time to waste. We must think big now.

Think big.

Think big.

Words have the potential to lose their meaning through overuse. Sometimes it seems as if everyone is talking about big thinking. Yet note how they are talking about it, what they mean when they say it . . . too often it is thinking big from a consumption point of view. For so many, thinking big is about being larger, about having more: more fame, more money, more power, more influence. Thinking big is not about quantity, about more. More is not expansive. Big thinking is expansive.

Big thinking is open and generous, discerning and judicious, yet not judgmental. Big thinking is not excessive, nor is it about the pursuit of excess. Rather, it is moderate.

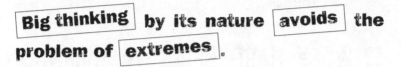

Big thinking by its nature avoids the problem of extremes.

Nothing is all good or all bad in this universe of contradictions. We fall into the dangerous trap of small thinking when we succumb to a belief in extremes, starting with a necessarily false belief in some universal infallibility, or worse still, our own.

To think expansively is to begin again and again at first principles, with the beginner's openness toward the world coupled with the wisdom of experience—our own and, as important, that of others.

To live in integrity is to be and to think and to act in the current of positive energy created by the expansiveness of big thinking.

What are your dreams, hopes, ambitions, and goals? Have small thoughts killed your aspirations? If so, whose small thoughts? Your own? Those of others?

Dream. Aspire. Do.

Statement of Integrity

I will be congruent in private and in public, in purpose and in action.
I will act in the spirit, light, and service of what I stand for.

13. WORK-HARD (BEING WARRIORS)

Before you can make choices in your life, there is an antecedent choice, an almost preconscious choice, that we all make: That is the choice between what is *easy* and what is *right*. It is this choice that distinguishes small thinking from big thinking. Can you guess which choice encompasses big thinking? If not, go back to the beginning of the book and start again. True, sometimes easy is also right, but don't confuse or inappropriately compound the two.

Thinking big is not necessarily incremental. You can't try it on for size. There's no test-drive, no *I'll-think-about-it-over-the-weekend*. To think big is to make a potentially radical and complete commitment to living fully—and, yes Virginia, it is hard work (Santa Claus is doubtful). To live by our hopes and dreams, to be driven by passion, is not easy, but it is right.

PASSION FUELS big things. To love the process (by which I mean the work of life) with the lightness of a beginner enables ACCOMPLISHMENT.

When we are inspired by what we do, work is not work as we used to think of it, as drudgery, as an *I've-got-to-do-this-but-soon-it-will-be-over* attitude. There is no more TGIF (thank god it's Friday). Work is not a forbidden four-letter word. When you work hard at something worthwhile, you naturally harvest the invigoration, the fulfillment, the meaning of work's brilliance.

Do you want to be doing what you're doing 20 years from now? If we are thinking big, the answer is yes, yes, yes. To build a remarkable business, to build a remarkable life, is not to worry about money but to do what we love. When it is passion we work for, then there is no other choice but to work hard.

Thirty years ago, Sandra Seagal experienced an epiphany during a therapy session with a nine-year-old girl. Sandra, a psychotherapist, became aware of certain sounds in the girl's voice: One was clear, while the other two seemed fainter, discordant with each other and with the first. Knowing something about the scientific research into frequencies in sound and light in the human body, Sandra suspected that what she was hearing might reveal a new way of assessing and developing balance and harmony in people. What Sandra had discovered were the three sounds within each one of us that indicate the balance and integration of our mental, emotional, and physical functioning, what has become known as the field of *human dynamics*. Sandra Seagal and her husband, David Horne (also a therapist), began to passionately pursue researching and refining this field of knowledge. Sandra was thinking big when she made her original discovery in a state of wide-openness to the knowledge the world offered, but the discovery was not the end of the challenge. It was the beginning of what has now been 30 years of hard work (and continuing to think big) to build the framework of understanding that supports and explains the fundamentals and nuances of human dynamics. We don't think big for one moment and then rest on our laurels. We think big; we work hard; then we think big and we work hard; then we think bigger; and so on.

When Jonathan Hunt decided, after 20 years as a financial planner, that he wanted to make a lifestyle change, to move his business online, so that he could travel and work from anywhere, he worked hard to pursue his dream. He created a new business architecture with an online service that informed and advised his clients in a timely, efficient way and even allowed them to make online transactions. In the beginning, he took on all the responsibilities of the business, because he was growing it on cash flow alone, no start-up money, no venture capital or private equity for a cushy start or a soft landing. He took care of sales, support, customer service, and training. His business grew. He worked harder. One day another financial planner asked to buy his system, and another, and then many others. Now Jonathan works exclusively for other financial planners instead of for consumers. He can travel. He can work (hard) from anywhere. He worked hard to get there.

To work hard, which we'll need to do when we're thinking big, we must cultivate the warrior within us (nothing to do with testosterone). We must train ourselves to be psychologically, intellectually, and physically capable to withstand the hard work we'll need to do and yet still be able to relax into life, to find the levity, the fun, to stay foolish. That is what it means to be a warrior.

Sandra Owens is a warrior. To see her now, in her shop in Vermont, surrounded by the gorgeous jewelry she has designed and created, it is hard to believe that at the age of 28 (about 20 years ago), she was told she would soon be in a wheelchair. After having her two children, Sandra's childhood scoliosis flared up so badly that X-rays of her spine looked more like a colony of mushrooms. She was plagued by constant and excruciating pain and could hardly walk. A doctor told her to get her affairs in order, because by the time she was 40 she'd be wheelchair bound. She couldn't afford the expensive and extensive medical care she was apparently going to require. And being the independent owner of a small jewelry shop, she was turned down for disability. Meanwhile, she had two small daughters and no house to speak of, as she and her husband were in the midst of building their house (with their own hands) while living in the garage as a temporary solution.

She felt like a cornered rat. "Being turned down for disability was the best thing that ever happened to me," she says now. "It closed off all the options except one—me. If there was a solution to my problems, it was me. I had to do for me, because no one else could. I was responsible for my own health."

Instead of giving up or giving in, Sandra fought. Lying on the floor one day she determined to exercise her back, to regain her strength. She pushed into the pain, relentlessly exercising her back when others weren't around to witness her contortions. One day she decided to try riding her bicycle again. She practically crawled out of her house, which was really just the garage where her family lived, dragging her bike with her. Alone on the quiet country road, she lay her bike down on the ground and lifted a leg over to straddle it. Slowly she righted the bicycle beneath her and began to coast down the hill. She couldn't pedal. It was too painful. As she reached the first intersection, still unable to pedal, she had a choice. Turn right and keep coasting downhill until pedaling might be possible, or stop and fall sideways off the bike and then make her way home, somehow. She kept going. After two miles of coasting, she found her ability to pedal. It wasn't pretty and it didn't feel good.

When you walk into Sandra Owens's shop now, you'll find a beautiful, strong, straight-backed woman, full of energy and a zeal for life, biking in the summer, tele-mark skiing (a challenging form of alpine skiing, with the *free heel* of cross-country skiing) in the winter.

Has she looked at an X-ray of her back lately? No. She doesn't need to—she feels great. Warriors take responsibility for their health, their fitness for life.

This book is about the psychological training you will do to become a warrior—about how to think big. That's not enough. You will also train intellectually in your chosen field and beyond. And last, but not at all least, you must train physically. No, this is not an exercise book and I'm not going to give you workout plans. But you will have great difficulty accomplishing big things if you are not healthy. It takes energy to accomplish big things in the world. Not to put too fine a point on it, if you don't mind your health, you may not be around long enough to finish the big things you've started. I still miss newscaster Tim Russert's insight and analysis.

The United States as a whole is fatter than ever, more out of shape and on too many drugs. Childhood obesity and sloth-induced diabetes are reaching epidemic proportions. The whole solution will never be found in a bottle, a pill, or a syringe—that's small thinking. We already have the solution: It's us—thinking big, if only we will take the responsibility. Just as slack thinking saps our emotional and intellectual strength, so, too, do lazy physical habits.

To do big things we need to be powerful warriors, psychologically, intellectually, and physically.

Yes, it stands to be repeated. When we are thinking big, we come together with others and train to do big things. Your workout partner may be as important to achieving your big dreams as is your study partner, your business partner, and your love partner.

How are you making yourself stronger every day?

With our strength and reserves, the future takes on a different hue.

When we are thinking small, we shrink from time's relentless path, hoping for something, anything really, other than the need to change our ways. We are weak in the face of the future bearing down on us.

When we are thinking big, time is a gorgeous horizon, hotly anticipated. We live, awakened, as Henry Thoreau put it, "by an infinite expectation of the dawn." When we are thoughtful and engaged; all things are possible, given time. We must be willing to test our dreams through the dialectic of thought and action. By the way, isn't *dialectic* a lovely word? In 8 letters it manages to capture both the idea of the back and forth of argument and the building process, so essential to big thinking, that occurs as a result of that collaborative engagement.

Small thinking avoids interesting, expressive words. Why learn something new when we already know enough to get by? Small thinking takes refuge in entrenched ideas and knee-jerk reactions, thereby avoiding the new or the difficult, a formula that guarantees we will achieve less than our potential.

We cannot, and need not, imagine the limits of our potential. Every day is possibility, if we have the energy to embrace it.

How do you replenish your energy, psychologically, intellectually, and physically?

Statement of Work

I am a warrior.

I will train to be strong psychologically, intellectually, and physically, so that I may have the fortitude to do the big things I am capable of.

21. HAVE FUN (YES, IT'S OKAY)

Life is absurd. To surrender to the silly is to learn to breathe. No breath, no life. Laugh, and the next mountain will crumble before you. Don't fight the obstacles. Move them. Embrace challenge. Playfulness is the hallmark of any great human activity; it inspires innovation and change, and it nourishes the mind as well as the body. How many times have you heard that laughter can prevent illness? It can, but it can do so much more. If there is no play in your life, in your home, in your work, it is a sure sign of *dis*-ease (maybe of disease, too), of decay.

The world is a funny place. Great minds run in great circles. If at first you succeed, hide your astonishment. If people listened to themselves more often, they'd talk less. Are these statements too general? All general statements are false. Think about it.

Why did the chicken cross the road? To get to the other side and pick up its copy of *The Think Big Manifesto* from the bookstore.

We know the true masters by their ability to see the humor in all things real and imagined. The ability to lighten up is essential to thinking big, for it is the hallmark of letting go of the need to control the world. We have no control. We are out of control. We can be terrified by this, or we can laugh at the amusement-park ride that is life. If we deny the importance of laughter, we will stifle our creativity. To recognize and find joy in the absurdity of life is as much a part of thinking big as is working hard.

Have fun and grow.

When was the last time you laughed until your stomach hurt? When was the last time you laughed so hard you cried?

Statement of Fun

I will embrace chaos and joy.

I will let go of the false notion of control and laugh at the inevitable absurdity of existence, mine above all.

34. REVOLUTION TIME (STOP WAITING FOR GODOT)

Thinking big means doing today what you could put off until tomorrow . . . if you were thinking small. Small thinking is waiting for the other—thing, person, event, day, month, millennium. There's no one to wait for. You are waiting for you.

Nobody who thinks big is thinking as big as they can. Procrastination is often just a way to make excuses for not thinking big: *I'll go to LA after this other thing comes together (if it does). I'll go on a diet after the holidays. I'll quit this job I hate only after I've found a new one (not that I'll have time to look). It's not a good time . . . I'll start in the fall.* Excusitis is a disease with symptoms—missed opportunities. And life, after all, is nothing but opportunities, one after another. Either you reach out and grab them, or you miss out on nothing less than your life.

So start now, because your life depends on it.

Grab life as it comes. In a 2005 commencement address at Stanford, Steve Jobs told a bit of the story of his life. He's a college dropout. Partway through, he realized he was wasting his adoptive parents' savings by pursuing studies he had no interest in. It wasn't that he didn't like education. He did. He audited classes subjects that interested him. Calligraphy, for example, was a course he pursued for a while. He took classes at random, following his passion, guided by intuition. For a time he couldn't connect the dots looking forward.

When we are follow ing our heart , we need to trust that the dots will connect.

When did you last learn something new just for fun? How has it applied in your life?

As we all know, Jobs eventually connected the dots in a big way . . . the Apple computer, the first computer that developed beautiful fonts and typography (which were then copied for the PC, of course). Even as I'm typing this manuscript on my (Apple) computer, I am able to choose from a host of gorgeous typefaces, and I have the big thinking of Steve Jobs to thank.

But that's not the end of the story. In 1985, Jobs was very publicly fired from Apple. Sounds like a good reason to mope. Instead, he says, he shed the heaviness of success and felt again the lightness of the beginner, the days of calligraphy, and following his passion. He founded NeXT (a computer platform development business) and Pixar (which produced movies such as *Toy Story*). The next five years of his life were his most creative. He loved what he did again. Not to mention that he fell in love with the woman who became his wife. Eventually, as we all know, he ended up back where he started, at Apple.

Steve Jobs credits his resilience to a quote he read when he was 17 years old. It went something like this (and he has no idea who said it, nor do I, although lots of people have said something similar): "If you live every day as if it were your last, someday you'll most certainly be right." He tried to live by that credo. And on any given day, if he looked in the mirror and thought to himself that he hadn't lived the past few days as if they were his last, then he knew he needed to change something.

We can all try to live each day as if it were our last, but Jobs knows what that really feels like from close up. In 2004, he was diagnosed with pancreatic cancer and was told he had three to six months to live, full stop. For a day he lived with that thought. Further tests revealed that he had a rare form of cancer that was both operable and curable, without the need for chemotherapy or radiation.

Jobs views his brush with death as a valuable life lesson. Death, he says, is the greatest invention. It is life's change agent. We all face our inevitable demise, and that has to make you think. Don't waste your life living someone else's. Your heart and intuition already know what you want to become. As Jobs says, we need only the courage to follow! It takes courage to think big.

It's heady stuff. Not for the fainthearted. It means taking risks. It means getting comfortable with being uncomfortable. You can mitigate the risks, but you can never totally avoid them. Because thinking big will keep putting you into new situations—it's funny how your heart just keeps wanting to do new things, if you let it be your guide.

Another thing, if you really want to get things done, stop procrastinating: Don't hang out with people who make an art of putting things off. If those close to you are moping, bitching, and complaining, you will, too. We all want to be like those around us. Don't surround yourself with people who are going to bring you down.

One more word about this whole *live-each-day-as-if-it-were-your-last* thing: It is *not* the same thing as living as if there is no tomorrow. It's not about emptying your bank account and spending everything, about eating everything in sight, about partying until the wee hours and never sleeping.

> LIVING each day to the FULLEST does not mean engaging in one final blowout. It means living in integrity, in AUTHENTICITY. It means being exactly who you are each day.

It means always pursuing your dreams, not wasting time on detours or holding patterns. Be on the true path you want to be on.

Life is ultimately a race against death. We don't know how long the race is going to last, but we all hope it's a long one. As with any race, we often need to be husbanding our resources. Our energy ebbs and flows. It must. We can't always be going 100 miles an hour, or at a snail's pace, for that matter.

It's common wisdom in running marathons that if you *go out* too fast (i.e., run too fast in the first miles of the race), then you will lose not only the time you gained at the beginning of the race, but much more at the end of the race. Here's one calculation you often hear: For every minute too fast in the first half, you lose 10 minutes off the back half. Whether or not that precise formula works for everyone, you get the picture. Maintaining reserves of energy doesn't mean we aren't giving something our all. Just the opposite: In fact, disciplined marathoners who can learn how much to hold back early and how much to give later are more focused on their end goal, on their dream, than the racer who spends everything in the first miles.

How is your race going? Are you already tired, or have you barely put in an effort yet?

In life, we don't have a choice about when the race starts. We can't wait until later. We're already in it. We've been in the race since the day we were born. It's up to us to achieve our dreams, to be heading in the right direction at the right pace, to maintain our energy, and to keep our focus on the goal. If you think you've waited too long, that there's no point, anyway, that it's too late to set a new pace—stop now and jettison that small thinking. Life is a race you can't give up on. There's no stepping off to the side and taking a break. It isn't over until it's over. It's never, ever too late to have dreams, to head toward them, to achieve them, to be happier.

So, if you still want to wait until tomorrow, or the next day, or next year, to do what your heart wants you to do . . . *don't*. The time to start thinking big is now. Sometimes, it's just about getting it done. Think big.

Be now. Find yourself in others and realize there is no *other*, only *we*. Live tomorrow today.

What have you been putting off? What can you do today instead of tomorrow?

Statement of Now

I will be now. I am now.

I will not wait for the other in the false security of excuses and procrastination.

I will do now.

VI.
WHEN-IS NOW

I, Michael Port, am thinking bigger about who I am and what I can do with others—*with you*. You *are* the revolution, not just a part of it. I am only one of a growing host of leaders. Don't look to me. Look to you.

The Think Big Revolution starts today and tomorrow. It started yesterday. This is its proclamation, its call to action, its inspiration, and its catalyst.

And remember: I love you very much (and not in a weird way) for being the big thinker you are now and the even bigger thinker you can and will be.

STATEMENTS OF THE THINK BIG REVOLUTION

Statement of Core

I will identify what I stand for through a concerted process of self-questioning and exploration to discover my core, the *what* that is so *me*.

I will make public what I stand for.

I will hold myself visibly accountable each day to its letter and spirit.

Statement of Independence

I will be comfortable with who I am right now and know that I am good enough.

I will use my innate talents and gifts to do big things in the world.

I will not give up in the face of others' fear or disbelief.

Statement of Collaboration

I will be a person others want to work with.

I will work with others without hidden or selfish intent to accomplish our mutual goals in the service of what each of us stands for.

Statement of Discomfort

I will not seek control.

I will make visible my purpose, make promises in its service, and take risks to fulfill my commitments.

Statement of Promises

I will be an authentic person, one whom others can rely on.

I will make hard promises that push me to the best of my capacity.

I will not try to fulfill. I will.

Statement of Submission

I am here to learn.

I will deliberately seek out wise and true teachers and submit to the authority of the constraints they create in the service of our goals.

Statement of Integrity

I will be congruent in private and in public, in purpose and in action.

I will act in the spirit, light, and service of what I stand for.

Statement of Work

I am a warrior.

I will train to be strong psychologically, intellectually, and physically, so that I may have the fortitude to do the big things I am capable of.

Statement of Fun

I will embrace chaos and joy.

I will let go of the false notion of control and laugh at the inevitable absurdity of existence, mine above all.

Statement of Now

I will be now. I am now.

I will not wait for the other in the false security of excuses and procrastination.

I will do now.